ELLENDER'S VISION:
The Lord of Her Heart

Lois Price

ISBN 978-1-63575-681-4 (Paperback)
ISBN 978-1-63575-683-8 (Hard Cover)
ISBN 978-1-63575-682-1 (Digital)

Christian Faith Publishing, Inc.
296 Chestnut Street
Meadville, PA 16335
www.christianfaithpublishing.com

Printed in the United States of America

Truman Austin &
Mary Ellender Jones
Married - Aug. 18, 1928

Amazing Courage—Ellender's Prayer

Lord, sometimes I face disappointment and challenges beyond my capability, and I am left afraid and worried. When I am fearful, let me seek Your strength. When I am anxious, give me faith. Keep me mindful, dear Lord, that with You by my side, I have nothing to fear.

Help me to be a grateful and courageous servant this day, and may I teach my children the ways of the Lord.

—Found in Ellender's Bible

Ellender Pillars, age three

High school graduation, eighth grade

Ellender

Mom's first home, 1909

High school class, Ellender's second

CONTENTS

Jones Family   1929-2016

1929-1937   Sybil Inez

Truman and Ellender, dating in Oklahoma (1928)

FOREWORD:
SANTA MONICA

Reading this book, floods my memories .

When I think of home is says "Santa Monica," for me going back to 1948. I was four years old and my mom moved my entire family of eight to Santa Monica. We were met by neighbors, our ages, who we immediately started playing with in the driveway. John Muir was the name of the elementary school that I was to attend kindergarten, it seemed so far. It was located two blocks down the alley and was scary, because I had never been away from my mom. Many friends from this school were the same friends thru Samohi, of course I made new ones along the way. The high school meant proms, dances and like the movie *American Graffiti*, a lot of time spent riding around in cars and going to drive inns to socialize, while eating French fries and drinking cokes. I cannot forget the wonderful days spent with friends at the beach, I would get so burnt, but it didn't matter. I love the beach to this day. Oh yeah, also some studying, if we had time.

My social life was our church, again from the earliest time I can remember, many friends at church. We had wonderful parties, meeting boys too and they had to go with us to church for us to be allowed to go out with them. We were all married in this church, so the memories go deep. It was amazing to have our family all involved in church, we all wanted to sit by our sister Jo, she was in a wheelchair.

It all happened in a wonderful town of Santa Monica, so grateful to mom for taking us there, making us safe and giving us such a good start to adulthood.

Trudy Jones Stanton

INTRODUCTION
TO THE JONES FAMILY

Santa Monica, California

Truman Austin Jones, father (deceased May 1944)
Mary Ellender Jones, mother (deceased August 25,1998)

Ellender was the daughter of Mini Gresham Pillars and Joseph Hall
Pillars. Her parents were dirt farmers in Oklahoma; they grew anything and everything that was green and would grow by seeds.

Ellender was the oldest of six children. She went to school when
possible and graduated from the eighth grade. In fact, she attended
a one-room schoolhouse, and she was the only student in the eighth
grade. This was in Scoby, Oklahoma, a small town between Wayne
and Paoli.

Ellender married a farm boy named Truman. She delivered
ten live babies in fifteen years. She buried two of her children, one
from polio and one from a breathing disorder. She helped her husband make a living by picking cotton, beans, peas, corn, or any farm
crop that needed picking. She delivered all her babies at home. She
cooked, cleaned, changed diapers, washed clothes, ironed, and babysat for other families just to help feed and keep a roof over her own
family's head.

When Ellender and Truman married, she had an eighth grade
education. She liked history best but struggled with math. She had
never paid the bills nor wrote a check until my father died in 1944.
She came from a primitive Baptist church background (better known
as Hard-Shell Baptist). Her parents were hardworking, uneducated

farmworkers. My grandfather could read but only had a third grade education.

Ellender was known as the widow woman with eight children from 1944 to the late '80s, when she married for the second time to Ed Stoner Sr. of West Los Angeles. Mom and Ed had seven years together before Ed died of a stroke at the age of eighty-five.

Ellender's goal in life was to see all her children married and to have a lot of grandchildren. When she died, she had total of sixty-nine grandchildren and great-grandchildren combined. While living in Santa Monica, she raised her children on welfare, ironing and babysitting for about seventeen years. Her hobbies were coin and stamp collecting (first-day-issue stamps) and crocheting.

She loved her church and was very active at Centinela Baptist Church of West Los Angeles from 1948 to 1983. She joined the First Baptist Church of West Los Angeles in 1984 and stayed active until her death in 1998. Ellender was a Rotarian, active with the senior women's club of West Los Angeles, served at church as a greeter on Sunday mornings, taught Sunday school, and sang in the choir.

Sybil Inez, first child
(born February 10, 1929;
deceased November 24, 1937)

Inez had polio in the early years of her life. She was just barely getting started in life, going to school, making friends; then she got this terrible disease, a disease with no cure. The doctors were at loss of what to do for these children. She was hospitalized for polio in Oklahoma City, and this was where she died. She had gone into surgery to repair the muscles in her legs and came out of surgery okay. But the nurse inserted an intravenous incorrectly, causing an air bubble to go to her heart, and she died at the age of nine.

Marjorie Lucile
(born October 25, 1930; deceased May 6, 2015)

The second child was with Inez. The day she took sick at school, Marge did not get sick. Everyone thought that Inez had a stomachache because she had a peach; the peaches were not ripe and still green. But when she got home from school, Inez had a high temperature, and also Ima Jo had a fever. Thank God Margie was doing well.

After Inez's death, Marge became the oldest, and she had to work hard to care for all the children that our mother kept having. Marge's choices were to change diapers or pick cotton. She picked cotton along with the men in the fields for many years of her young life.

When the family moved to Malibu, California, Marge became the mom to all the children so our mother could go to work. Marge went to school in Santa Monica, going and returning on a school bus each day. Her job on the bus was to care for her sisters and her brother until they reached home.

Marge was very shy and had always been told that children were seen but not heard, so she kept her opinion to herself and just did as she was told. The year Marge graduated from Santa Monica High school was the year our family moved to Santa Monica in 1948. Marge attended Santa Monica City College, which was a small building off Pico and Main Street downtown. This was where she met Jack La Vancil. Not only was he good-looking, but he owned a convertible car. They married in January 1951. Marge and Jack had four children. Two boys died at birth from hyaline membrane disease. Mari Kay and Jack Donald Jr. lived and were raised in the San Fernando Valley, California. Jack died 1955.

Marge married a second time to Ray Tefertiller on December 17, 2005. They were together for only one and a half year when Ray died on June 9, 2006. Marge died on May 6, 2015.

Allie (born June 18, 1932, only lived eighteen days)

The third child, Allie June, died eighteen days after birth from respiratory problems. No one really knew what caused her to stop breathing. Some said polio; some said she was struggling to breathe from the moment she took her first breath. A quiet family funeral was held in her memory. A marker was placed in the cemetery fifty-three years after her death.

Ima Jo
(born June 4, 1934; deceased September 6, 1999)

The fourth child, Jo, was three years old when she got sick with polio, a new disease that doctors and hospitals knew very little about. She became ill the same day as her sister Inez; both suffered from high fever. Doctors thought at first it was measles, but when the fever broke and the girls could not move their limbs, they were taken by ambulance to Oklahoma City and put into a polio children's ward.

Once Jo arrived in California, Jo was put into Rancho Los Amigos hospital polio ward, and she lived there for several years, from 1940 to 1950. When she was fifteen years old, the doctors told our mom to let her come home; there was nothing they could do for her now. After twenty-plus surgeries and her spending time in an iron lung, the doctors felt her progress had ceased to exist and that she probably wouldn't live to the age of twenty-one.

My mother would not accept this diagnosis from the doctors and said, "Bring her home. I'll care for her." A home teacher was provided to Ima Jo, and she excelled in her studies and graduated from Santa Monica High School (she did not attend the school but graduated with the senior class). She was given the opportunity to go to college. A driver was provided by the state welfare department. Again, Jo excelled in her studies. She had many, many friends and was voted Miss Spin-Drift (homecoming queen). She was also given a scholarship to a college of her choice. She chose Riverside Baptist College, where she met her future husband, Tom Gorrell. She married and had three children named Roxanne, Bill, and Dorothy. She also had seven grandchildren at her death in 1999. She was sixty-five years old. Jo spent her entire life in a wheelchair. She loved God, gave him all the glory for her achievements, was a motivational speaker for women's retreats and churches across the country.

Zelma Lou (born February 10, 1936)

Marge tells me that when Lou was a baby, she would cry a lot, and our dad would walk the floor with her and say, "Go to sleep, Loudy girl, go to sleep."

As Lou grew up, she helped mom a lot with all the siblings, especially with Jo. They were close in age, so they spent a lot of time together. Lou studied violin in junior high and high school. She was quiet, easygoing, and loved to please Mom. Marge says that Lou loved hot roasted peanuts. Daddy would go to the fields on Sunday afternoon and pick the peanuts, and Mom would roast them in the oven. The kids would sit on the front porch and eat those peanuts until they were stuffed.

Lou saw George working on a house one day as she was walking to school. He was a few years older than Lou and already a carpenter. She brought him home to meet Mom, and Lou and George were married on June 24, 1957. After Lou graduated from Santa Monica High School, they had six children: four girls and two boys (Jamie, Jody, Joel, Jess, Jana, and Jenny). They made their home in Kernville, California. She has grandchildren and great-grandchildren. The last count was thirty-five.

Eleanor (born February 8, 1938)

Nora was the youngest of the older girls, Mom's first set of children. Because Dad and Mom were so busy in the fields and also from taking care of two children with polio, I think maybe Nora was left out of a lot of things. She was the youngest of four girls, and Mom and Dad were moving a lot, working the fields, and did not have any place to call home.

Nora always felt bad because she was the only family member who didn't get a second name, and this was because when she was born, the doctor asked Daddy to name her. Dad said, "Allender" with his Oklahoma accent. The doctor thought he said *Eleanor*, and that's how she got her name. We've always called her Nora. When she was little, Daddy called her *Allner*, meaning "Ellender," so she was lucky to have Mother's name even though it didn't get on the birth certificate.

Nora graduated from Santa Monica High School and married a young man named Ronnie Sutherland in 1956. The marriage did not last long. They divorced, and while she was working, she met John Lester. She and John were married for forty-eight years. They have one son, Michael, and John passed away from heart failure in August 2008.

Nora is active in her church, Soaring Ministries, and makes her home in Camarillo, California. She is the prayer warrior for our family; she prays that none of our family or the world's family will be lost. We love each other, care for each other, and thank God for our family because of her faithfulness to prayer. She is strong, determined, faithful, trusting, and loves her God.

Scotty Buck (born December 26, 1939)

Buck is the only boy in our family. My father was so proud of his boy; he showed him off to everyone. After my father passed away in 1944, Buck was the only man in the house for many years.

As he grew, he really wanted to get away from all these girls. He started to go to Santa Monica Pier almost every day. He met some nice men down there, and they taught him to run the ski boats, to water-ski, and they helped him become a ship captain. After graduation from Santa Monica High School, Buck joined the coast guard for two years in active duty and several years as a reserve.

He made his home in the Marina del Rey, California. He moved to Fort Lauderdale, Florida, and started his own yacht brokerage business. He met Judy in Florida. They were married in Las Vegas, Nevada, on December 4, 1982. He and Judy continue to live in Fort Lauderdale, and also on the West Coast, Marina Del Rey, he can be found at all boat shows. His first love was the ocean; Mom always said his veins were filled with saltwater.

Doris Faye (born January 13, 1942)

Doris Faye is the eighth child. Mom always referred to her three youngest girls as her second set of children: the first set before Buck, the second after Buck. Doris was the older of the second set of girls.

Doris was very active in sports, and because she was tall and strong, she really helped a lot when it came to Jo's care. She could lift Jo, push her in her wheelchair, and help her to get dressed. Doris graduated from Santa Monica High School in 1959. Doris married

Calvin Lawson Taylor on August 1,1959, and together they had six children: Tracy, Calvin, Nora K, Aaron, Alex, and Ted.

They moved often, living in Simi Valley, Lake Isabella, Wofford Heights, and Ojai in California.

Calvin died in March of 1988. He was a fireman for the Los Angeles Fire Department.

Doris's oldest daughter, Tracy, also died, leaving three children. Doris has made her home in Bakersfield, California, for several years, helping raise her grandchildren. She never remarried. She has twenty-two grandchildren and eleven great-grandchildren. She worked for a counselor as an art therapist for two years with foster kids. She was a foster parent for fourteen years.

Doris makes her home in Camarillo, living with her daughter, son-in-law, and their children. Doris is the genealogist in the family. She has worked on the family history, collecting documents, pictures, and letters for more than thirty years.

Lois Maye (born March 5, 1943)

As the ninth child, a child who loved to be held, my sisters tell me that I would scream when they would put me down. I was very shy and didn't like men at all (except Jack and George), but even that took a while. I would hide in the closet when company came over.

I once pulled the cord of the iron while sitting under the ironing board. It was hot, and it came down and landed on the top of my left foot. I still have the scar from that terrible day; I don't remember one thing about it.

I didn't like school; I would have preferred just to stay home with Mom and Jo. I cried a lot and was scared of the teachers, scared of change, getting lost whatever I could think up next. I played the violin from fifth grade to tenth grade. I had to carry my violin with me wherever I went because it was too large to store in a locker at school, and the teacher would not let me leave it in the music room, afraid it might be stolen, so I carried it all day.

I met Dale Lingard in an English class at Santa Monica High School. We married after my graduation; it was July 7, 1961. We had three children together: Scott, Terri, and Kendra. We made our home in Culver City, California. Dale and I divorced in 1995, and I moved in with my mom to care for her until her death in 1998. I then moved to Corona, California, bought my first house on my own, and lived there until 2000.

I met Fawzi Abu-EI-Haj in 1999, and we married December 2, 2000. We lived in his house in Riverside, California. I bought a house in Bakersfield, California, as a second home because Fawzi was ill, and I would need a place to live. Fawzi passed July 1, 2011.

I moved to Camarillo to live with my sister Nora for a short time and met Steven Price in 2012. We were married July 8, 2012. We now make our home in Simi Valley, California. I have eight grand-children. I was active in the Red Hat Society for ten years and was part of my high school reunion committee for our fiftieth reunion. I just love staying in touch with friends and family. Steve and I travel in our motor home as often as possible. I volunteer at our church and enjoy women's Bible study.

Steve and I are archers, a part of the Conejo Valley archer asso-ciation, and competed in the 2016 Huntsman World Senior Games in Utah. I won a bronze and a silver medal in my age group.

Trudy Angela (born June 24, 1944)

Trudy is Mom's tenth and final child. Daddy had died just a month before Trudy was born, so her birth was a joy and sadness all in one. I always said that Trudy was very spoiled, being the last baby in the house; but of course, I was only a year older and very jealous of all the attention she was getting.

Doris, Trudy, and I were always good friends growing up. We knew each other's boyfriends and double-dated many times. Trudy liked school, and she had a lot of friends and got away with doing all the things that I would never have thought of doing, such as ditch-ing class or eating at Johnnie's Corner fast foods. The big thing was smoking and going to school dances.

Trudy met Ronnie Egner while attending Santa Monica High; she met him at our church. They married in 1963 for two short years and divorced. Tude, as we liked calling her, met James Meyer in 1968, and they were married in 1969. They have two beautiful daughters, Debra and Staci. Trudy divorced Jim after many years together and was on her own for several years. Then she met Bill Stanton in 2005, and they're now married. They make their home in Pismo Beach, California. Bill and Trudy love to travel. Tude loves the casino. She dabbles with the slot machines and wins a lot. I think I am still jealous. They enjoy eating out and walking down to the ocean to see the beautiful sunsets.

Trudy has four grandchildren and is so proud of them. She and Bill have recently remodeled their house in Shell Beach. It is really beautiful, and they will enjoy living there for many years to come.

SANTA MONICA WAS HOME

Santa Monica Pier, the Criterion Theater, Wilshire Boulevard, Lincoln Boulevard, Santa Monica High School, Pacific Ocean Park, John Adams or Lincoln Junior High, Pacific Palisades, Third Street shopping district, Santa Monica Venice Beach, Montana Avenue, Malibu, Santa Monica City College, Santa Monica Civic Auditorium. All great landmarks, all exciting vacation spots. But our family just called Santa Monica *home*.

We lived on Kensington Street between Pico and Ocean Park Boulevard. We lived on the west side of Lincoln, and I knew at a very early age that we lived on the poor side of Santa Monica. I knew also that if you didn't live north of Wilshire Boulevard, then most likely you were considered low income.

My family loved our house. Mom bought this house for twelve thousand dollars in 1948; she put five hundred dollars down and was able to have two lots. One lot was for the house; the other lot was for the garden. Mom grew everything in those garden: flowers, vegetables, grapes and berries, green beans, tomatoes, celery, corn. We all worked the garden, and Mom would can all the food so that it would last through the winter. We had a dirt cellar under the house, and we stored all the canned goods down in that cool, dry storage area.

We had a woodburning fireplace and a dog named Bounce who loved to curl up in front of that fireplace at night. We had a lot of neighbor kids to play with. We had roller skates, bicycles, a croquet set, a volleyball; we didn't need anything else. We had great Sunday afternoon dinners with fifteen to twenty people almost every Sunday. We all sat down together with friends and neighbors and gave thanks for all our blessings and the food that was provided.

We had one telephone for everyone in the house to use and one old typewriter that we could use for our homework. Our milk was delivered to our front door by Edgemar Farms. Helms Bakery trucks came to the front of our house with pastries, pies, bread, cookies, and the best chocolate brownies I have ever eaten.

When we were teenagers, we found out what pizza was and were able to eat at the very first McDonalds on Lincoln Boulevard. We walked to school, to the dentist's office, to shop at the Third Street mall. Our refrigerator was not frost-free and no ice maker; we used ice trays that were metal. We went to church every Sunday. We always took our boyfriends to church with us, both Sunday morning and Sunday evening.

Santa Monica was a great place to live and to grow up in. We had everything we needed, and we loved going to Pacific Ocean Park, watching the fireworks on the Fourth of July from the Fourth Street Park. The fireworks were shot off at the Santa Monica Pier. Criterion Theater had really good movies, and when we could save up enough money, we all would walk together all the way downtown to see Elvis, or John Wayne, or Elizabeth Taylor. We saved S&H Green Stamps, and Mom had a coin collection. Mom could watch TV on Saturday night, *Hometown Jamboree* with Tennessee Ernie Ford and Red Skelton.

Our life was simple. We didn't worry about drugs or pot, no one had tattoos, and most girls didn't even pierce their ears until they were eighteen. We had seventy-eight records and forty-five singles to play on a record player. We liked jumping rope and playing blinds man's bluff after dark. The '50s were a great time to grow up in. We were so blessed to live in Santa Monica. We were never concerned about all the landmarks, and we just called this place home.

Family Group Record

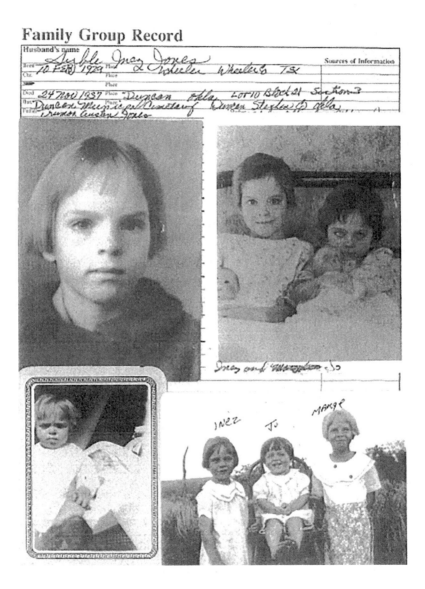

CHAPTER 1

Ellender's Story Told by Ellender

1997

My name is Mary Ellender. My nickname in my later years was Jonesy. My neighbor lady started calling me Jonesy in the early '50s, and it just stuck. I was born on July 19, 1909, in Colton County of Oklahoma in Randlett. This was north and east of Wichita Falls, Texas. My first remembrances are on the Guthrie Place, east and south of Lawton, Oklahoma.

My grandparents' names are Mathew Allen Pillars and Mary Catherine Williams. My parents were Mary Minnie Gresham (born September 27, 1889) and Joseph Hall Pillars (born in Alma, Arkansas, on March 7, 1890, in Crawford County). They were dirt farmers. I had one sister, Velma Laura. She was born in Lawton, Oklahoma, on May 25, 1914. I also had four brothers; Joe Herald was the youngest. He was born July 28, 1927, in Duncan, Oklahoma, a part of Wheeler County. Glen Cecil was born in Wayne, Oklahoma, on June 7, 1923, a part of Rosedale McClain County. David Odell was born in Lawton, Oklahoma, on January 10, 1917. And Raymond Allen was born August 1, 1911 in Randlett, Oklahoma, in Colton County.

I was about six-year-old, and I remember the Guthrie House. It was just wood, had two rooms, and it had a porch. We had some livestock, a few cows, and my daddy worked the land. We had rows and rows of onion, turnips, and corn. I remember hanging clothes on a barbed-wire fence that was hung around the side of the house. My mom would scrub the clothes in a wooden water tub and hang them to dry on this wire fence. Then a big wind would come up, and the clothes would go flying across the dirt. My mom and I would run after the clothes, wash them again, and again hang them on that fence to dry. My daddy would go out to the artesian well in a wagon that was pulled by two horses. The wagon held three wooden barrels, and he would bring us water to cook and clean.

One day we thought we were seeing a large formation of geese flying over our heads, but then we heard the noise of a motor. Daddy told me that they were airplanes. This was the first time I had ever seen an airplane, and I couldn't imagine how it stayed up in the air. I went to a one-room schoolhouse, and my teacher was Ms. Guthrie. She came to the school with a horse and buggy; she was nice lady. One day, we had a snowstorm, and my mom did not want me to miss school, and she sent me walking to that school building. I couldn't see very well because of the snowstorm. I tried to cut across the pasture, but I got lost in the large haystacks. I was walking around and around the haystacks and couldn't find my way out. My daddy was tending the stock, and when he returned to the house, he came looking for me. When he found me, my hands and feet were frostbitten. My daddy washed them with snow, and he carried me back to the house.

I must have been seven or eight when we moved to Chacatow, Oklahoma. When World War I broke out, my daddy thought that he would have to go to war. This was about 1915. My grandparents lived at Soper, Oklahoma. My dad thought that we should move in with them so they could help Momma with the kids. My grandfather was a minister of the Landmark Baptist Church, and he was also a farmer. We were able to move everything we had in one wagon. I do remember having to walk a long way alongside the wagon, and I had to help tend to the baby brother David. We had to walk up a long hill, and David didn't want to walk, so I had to carry him. Daddy let us sit in the wagon when we got to the top of the hill. My back and my feet were hurting so much I curled up in a ball and fell asleep. This was a two-day trip.

My grandfather Mathew Allen was a gambler and a blacksmith in his early years before becoming a minister and settled down to a family life. It was told that my grandmother Mary Catherine was the best dancer in the county.

When we arrived in Soper to my grandparents' home, we found a log cabin with two rooms, a large porch across the front, and two rooms across the back (they called them side rooms). My daddy did not go to war because he had so many kids, and he could farm. We stayed at this place, and Daddy helped Grandpa work the land. They grew all our food: corn, sweet potatoes, and onions. We had chickens, two cows, and a goat.

My daddy bought two horses to help pull the plow. One was a young horse, probably one or two years old, and we called him Charley. Then later he bought a dapple-gray horse, and they called him Judd. My daddy was very proud that he could have two horses. These horses loved watermelon, and when the melons came in season, those horses would come right up to the porch and eat watermelon right out of our hands.

My daddy was picking cotton for a man, and he had a Hupmobile. This was the first car I had ever seen. My mother was taking me to Texas to see her brother Quincy and his wife, Ruby. This man drove us to the train depot. I saw a car and a train for the first time on the same day.

While we lived in Soper, we were able to go to school at the Nelson place. We carried our lunch, which was sometimes biscuits or corn bread. Mom would ask us to pick up peach seeds along the way and take them to the school because of the war. They were collecting these seeds and pressing them into some kind of gas.

While we were at this school, we caught a disease called the seven-day itch. We caught it from the doctor's kids who also attended the school. Mother boiled poke roots and bathed us in it with sulfur. Our underclothes were as yellow as sulfur could be. The teacher at this school was called Ms. Summers, and she became a family friend.

My daddy was not happy living in Soper. He said the land was cut up too much, so he bought a second wagon in a town called Antlers. The whole family went to town, and Daddy had a family picture taken of us. In August of that year, about 1920—I believe I was eleven or twelve—we moved with two wagons, two horses, four cows, and our few pieces of furniture, and headed for Rosedale. Daddy had a sister, Annie, who was his oldest sister, and her husband, George William. They had a daughter named Betty. They lived in Rosedale, and Daddy felt that he could find work in this town.

We lived in an army tent. It was large and had sides that rolled up. We had a pail of water in the center of the tent, dirt floors, and we lived there through the winter and into January. Daddy wanted me to go to school, so we moved again to Indian lease land, and I was able to start school again in Scoby; this place was between Wayne and Paoli.

And we lived on this land for four years so that I could finish school in the eighth grade. I was the only student in the eighth grade. This was a one-room schoolhouse. Getting to school was not always easy. We had to cross through a pasture of land that was owned by a man named Hamer. The pasture was full of large trees and a large pond in the center, so we had to walk a lot farther to get around that pond. I can remember how cold it got in the winter, crossing that pasture and seeing the frozen lake, but I just wanted to go to school. My teacher was named Ms. Pegg, and she was nice to me. This is the school where I met Jess Prater. Jess was later my brother-in-law, but at this time, he was my first boyfriend. We didn't call them boyfriends in those days; my mom called him my beau. My brother David started to school here also. He was left-handed, and the teacher was not happy about it. She tried and tried to get him to use his right hand. One day she was so unhappy about it that she threw an ink bottle at him. The ink went everywhere, and this made her even madder.

Because my grandfather was a minister, the teacher asked him to preach one night at the school. His church was called primitive Baptist (we called it the old hard-shell preaching). He read the Twenty-Third Psalm from the Bible. The next day, while in class,

Ms. Pegg said that was the first time she had heard anyone read the Twenty-Third Psalm correctly.

A few weeks before my brother Glen was born in 1923, my daddy took us to a program at the school. It was evening, and we had to cross that pasture again. As we began to come home, a rainstorm came, and it rained so hard that it was hard to see. Daddy took us through the corn rows so it would be easier to go in a straight line. Daddy had Velma's hand, Raymond behind him and then me. I had my coat covering my head because it was hailing so hard. Daddy was carrying the lantern, so when we made it home, he sat the lantern on the porch. The next morning, the lantern was in many pieces, scattered on the porch. Daddy said that we made it home just in time.

Another time, we went to school in the evening for a program. Again, my dad took us kids; and this time, he carried his gun. We didn't know what he was going to do with this gun, and there was a lot of talk about it. But on the way home from that program, we stopped near that big pond, and Daddy started shooting the ducks sitting in the water. He got two or three before most of them flew away. We gathered up those ducks, took them home, and cleaned them for our dinner the next day. I believe that my uncle Judd was with us that evening. Uncle Judd was my mother's oldest brother. I remember being glad that my dad did not take the gun to shoot my teacher. If I remember right, you were not supposed to shoot animals on the Indian lease land.

My dad wanted me to continue school; but in order to go to the next grade, I would have to ride the horse to school, and Daddy said no to that, so we moved again. Grandpa Pillars had a brother who lived in Duncan. We moved to Duncan, and my parents rented a small place there. We moved in two wagons. Daddy was in one wagon, and Mom in the second wagon. Raymond and I took turns guarding the cows and the goat until we arrived in Duncan. The best part was that I could go to a new school west of Empire, a consolidated school. It was one large room, and the building was two stories high and was made of red brick. My class was upstairs on the eighth floor through the twelfth grade. I studied algebra, history, English, and geography. By now, I was so far behind in my schoolwork. I failed my math class, but I was first in English and history. This was when I met Lois Smith. She became my friend, and she helped me catch up in my math class.

I was in my second year of school in Empire when Jess Prater also moved to Duncan and began classes at our school, and he became the bus driver. Lois was seeing a boy named Truman Jones; I was seeing a boy named Charley Yates. Lois introduced me to Truman, and he came to my house the next day and asked my daddy if he could see me. Two years later, Truman and I married in Comanche, Oklahoma, and we had to live with my parents until we could get enough money to move to Texas to find work. Jess Prater married Truman's sister named Georgie Jones. Lois Smith married Truman's brother Emmett Jones. One of my best friends was Myrtle; she later died from measles.

Now, as I recall the story of my mother's wedding night, she and my dad, Truman, had gone to the county fair outside of town, and they decided to get married. So they went to the justice of peace, and they got married. When they got back to my grandfather's place, Grandma and Grandpa were sleeping in one room, also known as the kitchen, and Velma was sleeping on a mattress on the floor of the second room. Ellender told her mom and dad that she and Truman had just gotten married, so Grandpa got out of bed, went to the next room, and told Velma to get out of that bed because Ellender and Truman just got married. Velma had to go outside and sleep on the front porch with the boys. As I understand the story, my Aunt Velma didn't speak to my mother for a very long time because she had to sleep outside with the boys.

Margie Remembers Grandma and Grandpa Jones

Ellender and Truman left Texas, where they had found work in the fields, and they headed for Duncan, Oklahoma, to a place called the Willerford Farm several miles outside the city limits. It was late in the year 1936. Truman drove his family there in a wagon pulled by a team of horses.

As I was told this story by my sister Marge, she said, "Grandma Jones was a very mean woman. This old woman was mad at the entire world. She never had a good thing to say about anyone or anything." Elmer Rufus and Lilly Bell Jones were my father's parents. They raised five children: two boys and three girls (Emmitt, Truman, Addie, Willie, and Georgie). Their life was really hard living in the middle of the dust bowl. Oklahoma was hot, dry, and dusty most of the time.

The women washed the clothes on a scrubboard using a metal washtub. They cooked the food, tended the animals, gathered the eggs, slaughtered and cooked the chicken, and tried to scrap enough money together to buy sugar, molasses, blankets, and salt. Anything else they ate had to come out of their own garden or from the animals they raised. The men plowed the fields, planting the crops and working sunup to sundown. It was no wonder that Lilly Bell was tired and angry all the time.

When Ellender and Truman arrived at the Willerford Farm, they found the Joneses' house and had hoped to stay awhile, just until they could find another farm that needed pickers, or maybe find any work. On this particular day, Rufus had gone down to the corner to get a drink with some of the local men. The place was called Spit and Widow Corner. The old men would sit on chairs outside the bar, drink, and watch the widowed women and wonder whom they might get hitched up with.

When dinnertime came, Grandma Jones would go out to the porch and start yelling at the top of her voice, "ELLLLLMER, GET HOME NOW!" When he heard this yelling, he would spit out his chewing tobacco and begin the slow walk back to the house. When Rufus arrived home, Lilly Bell would be waiting for him, yelling about him staring at the women, chewing that terrible tobacco, and talking religion. She had his dinner waiting for him on the table. He would sit down and eat and not say one word to her.

Ellender had four children at this time: Inez, Marge, Ima Jo, and a new baby girl named Zelma Lou. Baby Allie June had died of a breathing disorder. Inez and Jo both had polio. Inez had to wear heavy metal braces on her legs and used wood crutches to try to walk. She was very frail. Grandma Jones would not let the sick children come into her house. She would say, "Just leave them out on the porch. No use everyone getting sick." Ellender was exhausted from the harsh weather conditions, sick children, a new baby, and a mother-in-law who was very hard to deal with. In the small town, they had just a short walk from the house to the corner store. The store had an icebox; it was such a luxury to be able to purchase a block of ice.

Grandma Jones gave Margie twenty-five cents and told her to take Inez down to that store and carry back a block of ice. This may seem simple, but Inez could barely walk with those heavy braces on, and it was very difficult for her to walk that far. But the girls did what they were told and went for the ice.

The Willerford house was not large but nice. It had a screened-in porch to keep the insects out, and some of the family members slept there on the porch. The house had a fireplace, three large wood tables and three chairs, two bedrooms, and their water came from a cistern out on the back porch. A bucket hung on a rope and was dropped down into a deep hole. They pulled the water up in that bucket; it was used for drinking, washing clothes, and bathing. The clothes were hung on a clothesline to dry. They had a cow that just wandered around the front of the house, and when the wind would whip up, the clothes would blow around, and that cow would chase those clothes. Sometimes he would knock the clothes to the ground, and they would have to be washed again.

Lilly Bell never washed her hair, not ever with soap and water. She used white cornmeal that she had made herself. She would dust it in her hair and use a small comb and work the dry dust through her hair, removing the oil and dirt. She spent many hours, mostly the evening hours, combing her very long hair.

Truman could not find work. They had no place to go and had two very sick children. She, Grandma Jones, wanted them to find another place to live, but Inez was very ill and needed to be hospitalized. The local doctor put Inez in the hospital in Oklahoma City. The doctor was hoping to stop the muscle from deteriorating. The surgery went well, but a nurse who was caring for Inez put an intravenous line in her arm. She made a mistake with the drip, and an air bubble formed in the line, went into Inez heart, and she died.

Inez's body was brought back to Duncan to Grandma Jones's house. She was laid in a casket, put on the table in the living room, and the relatives came for three days to say their good-bye and express their sympathy to Truman and Ellender. Inez was buried in Duncan. With no money for a headstone, Ellender just remembered the spot. She said she would never forget where they laid this child.

Marge Was Born in a Turkey House

Shamrock, Texas, 1930
The Tilden Ranch

Truman was working the fields. Ellender's second child was due any time, and they needed a place to live. On this ranch, they had raised turkeys, and that old turkey house was now empty. It was a prairie building with wood slates, dirt floors, no windows, and just had screen mesh over the window openings. Truman and Ellender scrubbed this old building, and they moved into the turkey house. They had no furniture, so neighbors and family gave them a few pieces of furniture: a bed, two chairs, and a wood table. Truman built a stone fireplace, and they pulled water out of a well close by. Marge Lucile was born in this turkey house, and they lived in this condition for almost five years.

Marge received her first Christmas present while living in the turkey house. It was a wooden box with a rubber ball and some jacks inside this box. Note, she kept this gift until her death in 2015. She still has the box with the ball in it; the jacks were lost.

Shamrock, known also as Twitty and also as Wheeler County, Texas, was where Marge, Ima Jo, and Lou were born. Then the family moved once again to Duncan, Oklahoma, in Stephens County, where Eleanor (Nora) and Scotty Buck were born. Nora was born on February 8, 1938, and Buck on December 26, 1939. Ima Jo was getting sicker and sicker. Her body would twist like a pretzel, she could not walk, and she was in and out of the hospital in Duncan, Oklahoma.

Truman was sharecropping on a farm in Duncan and took Jo to the Oklahoma City hospital as many times as needed. It was now 1940, and the doctors told Ellender and Truman that they needed to take Jo to the polio hospital in California. It is called Rancho Los Amigos hospital in Downey. The crops were failing, and they had no money—how would they get Jo to California? Ellender was also pregnant with her eighth child. They borrowed a car, a '35 Oldsmobile, and they talked to Sam Sherrill, Truman's friend, to go with them and all the children. This would be a very long drive to California. The year was now 1941.

There was no money to pay the farm owner for the crops that had failed due to horrible weather. Ellender had worked hard all year canning the crops that they were able to gather, rows and rows of fruit jars with corn, peas, onions, potatoes, tomatoes, okra, and green beans. Truman worked out a deal with the farm owner: he gave him all the food that had been canned for the payment that was owed. Now they were free to move once again, but this time, they were heading for California.

The Long Drive to California

The death certificate said polio, but Inez did not die from polio, though it was polio related. She was nine years old. She wore braces on her legs and was suffering with muscle deterioration. Her body was twisting into the shape of a *U*. The doctors told Mom that Inez needed surgery to stop the pain and to stop the muscle from deteriorating more. Inez went into surgery, and she was so frail. The surgery went well, the doctors said, but a nurse made a mistake with the intravenous line to her arm. Too much air got into the lines, and Inez's heart stopped. She died on November 24, 1937. This was Mom and Dad's first child.

Ellender and Truman took Inez's body home from the hospital, laid her on a table in the middle of the room at Grandma and

Grandpa Jones's house. She needed to be buried, but family and friends wanted to say good-bye. There was a wake for two days; then her body was buried in an unmarked grave in Oklahoma. All the money went to pay for the surgery, so they had no money for a headstone. Ellender studied the area of the grave site carefully and quietly. She looked for trees and other identification markers. She didn't want to forget where Inez's final resting place was. Ellender had no time to grieve. Ima Jo was still in the hospital with polio; she needed Mom's attention now.

Ellender and Truman's second child, Allie June, died. She had respiratory problems and only lived for eighteen days. Marge was seven years old, and Lou was one year old. Ima Jo was three years old and was also in the hospital with polio. What a desperate time for this family, so much sadness, heartache, and total desperation.

The early thirties was the time of the dust bowl. Polio was everywhere, and doctors were lost as to the treatment; it was all guesswork. Mom was desperate for help. She was just trying to keep her emotions intact, if that could be humanly possible. She was so afraid for Marge and Lou—how could she keep them from getting polio? No one knew how the kids got sick. They just woke one day with high fevers, aching all over, sick to their stomachs. No one was safe from this disease, yet some got it, and some didn't.

The hospital released Jo to Mom and Dad in just a few months. The doctors said that they had done all they could. Now it would just take time to find out the extent of the damage that the polio was doing to Jo.

Mom and Dad worked the fields of cotton, making a dollar a day. Marge was about nine years old now and was caring for the children. It was hard work for a nine-year-old child. The days were long, the ground was hot and dusty, and there was no place for the children to play. They moved from farm to farm, trying to find work. They had no home to call their own, and Mom was now pregnant with Eleanor. She was tired, Jo was sick, and Daddy decided to go to Soper, Oklahoma, where his parents lived. They needed a place to live, and they had no other choice. The house was old, made of wood, had no paint on it, no insulation. The porch was made of wood slates, and you could see down to the dirt between the spaces of each plank.

When they arrived in Soper, Mrs. Jones (our grandmother), my father's mother, came to her door and said, "You can't come in this house with that sick child." She was afraid of the polio. They had no place to go. The children were tired, hungry, and needed to sleep. It was cold and windy. They had brought some blankets with them, and they wrapped the children and bedded them down on the front porch; no one was allowed in the house.

Ellender used a large metal tub out front of the house to bathe the children. They ate their meals on the front porch or stairs, and they lived this way for about a month's time, until Daddy was able to find work in another town. The family continued to move from town to town, farm to farm, finding work of any kind. They picked cotton, corn, sweet potatoes, and onions. Whatever the crop was, Mom and Daddy would pick it. Jo was getting worse; she was not able to walk. Marge and Lou carried her most of the time, and Mom and Daddy would care for her at night. The work never stopped. Even though you were tired, there were always clothes to wash, butter to churn, cows to milk, meals to cook, sick children to care for.

In 1939, Scotty Buck was born. My dad was so happy to finally have a son. My mom told us great stories about our dad showing off his son to everyone who would stop and listen, four girls and one boy. Jo was in and out of the hospital. She was having problems breathing, and her back was so weak and was no longer holding up her body. The doctors told Mom and Dad that Jo must be taken to Los Angeles, California, to the cripple children's hospital in Downey, California. They should get her there as soon as possible, or she might die.

Truman borrowed a '35 Oldsmobile from a friend. It was black and had wool seat covers. He carried a canvas water bag on the front of the car for the radiator, and they made the decision to drive the entire family to California. Mom, Ellender, bought a loaf of bread and a stick of baloney. Daddy had ten dollars in his pocket. They put all their possessions in a small wooden trailer attached to the back of the car. A feather mattress was tied to the top of the car. They laid

Jo across the backseat and used the back of the seat to support her body. Marge, Lou, and Nora sat on the edge of the backseat just in front of Jo. Bucky was a year old and sat on Mom's lap. Mom sat in the middle of the front seat. Daddy was driving, and his friend Sam Sherrill came along with them. They would definitely need help with driving, caring for the kids, and what if that car broke down? They drove one entire day; then Daddy pulled alongside the road. He put the mattress on the ground; this was where Mom, Bucky, Daddy, and Jo would sleep for the night. Daddy built a small fire and made some coffee. Sam Sherrill and the other children wrapped themselves in blankets and lay on the ground next to the mattress. They ate bread and baloney for all meals. The second day, Daddy worked a farm field along with Sam Sherrill all day long and made enough money for gas and a little food.

This had to be the trip from hell. The girls sat on the edge of the wool seats all day, never being able to lean back and support their back in any way. When they got tired, they laid their heads on their arms across the back of the front seat and slept whenever they could. Jo couldn't see anything except the back of her sisters. It was hot and dusty, but Jo didn't complain. Where do folks find the strength and the courage to make such a desperate journey? I guess when you have no choice, you just do what you have to do.

Mom continued the story about when they were somewhere outside of Phoenix. They were driving along, and Daddy noticed a tire passing him on the left side of the car, just a tire rolling along by itself. Daddy said, "Look there, some fool has lost his tire." It didn't take long before he realized that it was his tire; he was the fool. The back left tire had come off, and the car was being held up by the wheel of the small trailer that they were pulling. There was no money to fix the tire, so once again, the family had to stop and work the fields to earn enough money to replace the tire. Food was almost gone, and the wool seats were so itchy and dusty. Mom said we needed to find a place to spend the night, some kind of motel or lodging, just one night to bathe. Everyone needed a hot meal and get a decent night's sleep.

They found a small town outside of Phoenix and pulled into a place that had rooms to rent. They entered the room that was for rent, and Ellender said, "Oh no, we can't stay here." There were fleas everywhere, millions of them. No way could the children come into this room for the night or even one minute.

They returned to the car and continued toward California. Finally, they reached the California coast on the sixth. On the day of the third week, they were in Santa Monica, California, a place they had heard about but could never imagine ever seeing. Daddy pulled up and stopped the car along the beach. He picked Jo up off the backseat, and everyone got out of the car just to see the most incredible sight that they could ever imagine. It was the Pacific Ocean, waves crashing down on rocks bigger than the car. The horizon just went forever. These cotton pickers couldn't believe their eyes. They were tired and hungry. After an hour of just watching with unbelief, they headed north on Highway 1 to a place called Malibu, also known as Pacific Palisades, also known as Malibu La Costa and the Santa Monica rural.

This was where they found Grandma and Grandpa Pillars, my mom's parents, who were waiting for them with a hot meal and homemade biscuits, bacon, eggs, and cantaloupe. This was the first hot meal they had eaten in about three weeks, and they were very grateful for it. My grandparents had driven down from Northern California, where they had been working at a farm, to meet Truman and Ellender and help them with the children so they could put Jo in Rancho Los Amigos hospital.

The house they were renting was owned by the Pippenberg family. This family owned two houses, and the one they were staying in was at the top of a hill. The area was called Pacific Palisades, also the Santa Monica rural. This was the house where Doris was born. It was hard for the kids to walk so far down the hill to catch a bus for school, so the Pippenberg family offered Mom and Dad a house to rent in Los Flores Canyon. This was the house where Lois was born in 1943 and Trudy was born in 1944.

We referred to this house as the *Pippenberg house*. Just a sidenote here:

1. Doris took Mom back to Oklahoma about 1985. They found the spot where Inez was buried, and they placed a small headstone. Even through all the years that had passed, Mom remembered where she buried Inez.

2. In 1942, Daddy bought that four-door sedan '35 Oldsmobile for $236.36, putting down a payment of $60.00 and paid $15.68 a month until it was paid in full in about eighteen months.

Sybil Inez Jones, Mom's eldest child

My father—Truman Austin Jones

Daddy balanced Jo in the fender of the car before
leaving to Rancho Los Amigos Hospital.

CHAPTER 2

The Pippenberg House

The house set back off the road. It was huge, like a big wood box, no real style of shape. It was made of old wood, and it was not painted, just the old weathered look. If you were looking at this house from the road, you would see a dirt driveway, deep ruts, and rocks that were small enough to drive over. The house was set one hundred feet from the road and had a staircase that had thirty-five steps and two landings. The stairs were so worn and warped, and you could see the nails pulling out of the wood. There were twenty-five steps and then a landing that measured about four-by-four feet with a wood rail. Then there were ten more steps and another landing that put you in front of the front door. The bedrooms for the older children were downstairs, a large room with a lot of beds; and Marge, Lou, Nora, and Buck slept downstairs. When you entered the large room upstairs, you could see a black potbelly stove in the middle of the room. Several chairs were around the wall. There was a large room to the right of the living room; this was the kitchen. It had a large black-and-white stove, and my mom would make the best homemade biscuits in that stove. Most of the memories I have of my mother at this time in my life was her standing and cooking at this stove, a rough, rustic table set off to the right of the stove and had six wooden chairs. The back of the chairs were rounded with spindle supports at the center. They were partially painted with different colors, and most of

49

the paint had worn off. The two last rooms in the house were bedrooms upstairs. My mom slept in one room, and the three younger girls slept in one bed in the second room.

This house was not insulated, and I remember that some of the wood slates had warped, and you could see through them to the outside. There was no bathroom in this house. Instead, we had an outhouse. It was a four-by-four wooden outhouse with a toilet that had a wooden seat on it. It was located about twenty-five feet from the back door and up a small hill. Sometimes we would find snakes around the outhouse, so my mom would take the broom and check the area in the mornings when we would get out of bed. We were too scared to use this outhouse at night, so Mom would put a metal bucket by the back door, and we could use that if we could not wait till morning.

On top of this house was a huge water tank. This house was not hooked up to plumbing, and the water was brought to the house by a water truck that came once a week and filled the water on top of the house. My mom would heat the water on the stove for our bath. Our bathtub was a large metal tub that Mom would put in the center of the kitchen floor, and we took a bath on Saturdays. Of course, everyone used the same water. Mom would add some new hot water for each person, and the three small girls bathed together at the end of the line.

The landscaping was very sparse. Geraniums of all colors grew wild along the hillside. Hollyhocks were scattered across the front of the house. There was no real plan for these plants, just a gift from God. We didn't water them. My mom would say, "If God wants them watered, he will make it rain." So they were not healthy-looking plants, just old and dirty. The hollyhock was a magical plant because the flowers could be transformed into a wonderful magic doll. This plant had one straight stalk from the ground up, and in the spring, these hard round buds would form on the stalk. When the bud would burst open into a beautiful magic doll dress—only in our minds, of course—the flower was a bell shape with a lovely, lacey turned-up edge. We would pop off one of the buds, making sure the stem was still attached, and push the stem into the top of the flower.

Voila! A lovely dancing doll or a floating angel. Our minds were at work overtime, playing with the flowers and creating a world all of our own.

Why was this house so important in my life? It is because I was born in this house, also my sister Trudy. This house was located in Malibu up the Los Flores Canyon, and it was up the road from the Malibu courthouse, where my father was killed. He was digging a hole for a septic system near the Malibu courthouse, next to the La Costa Restaurant. It was my father's turn in the hole. He climbed down the ladder about twenty-five feet when the hole caved in on him and suffocated him before they could get him out. He died on May 1944. My sister Trudy was born on June 1944.

My parents found this house in 1941. My mom worked for Mrs. Pippenberg as a housekeeper in the Malibu area. She rented this place to my mom and dad because they had a lot of children, five and one on the way. The house was large enough to invite my grandparents Minnie and Joseph Pillars; they lived with us for a short time. We moved away from this house when I was five years old. We moved to Santa Monica in 1948.

I remember some really fun times in the Pippenberg house. We would tie tin cans to our shoes and walk on the cans down the canyon road. This would make a loud echo. It was noisy, and it made us laugh. We found frogs that lived along the creek that ran along the side of the road. The water ran about a foot deep all the time, so we could walk on the rocks, and we built small dams to catch pollywogs and frogs. We had a dog; his name was Bounce. He was a brown-and-white mutt. He would disappear sometimes; we knew he was at the beach. He ran off every day to swim in the ocean. Years later, my brother said that he swam in the ocean to keep the fleas off him. I don't ever remember giving him a bath, but Mom allowed him into the house, and he slept pretty much wherever he wanted. We really loved that dog. We had a lot of cats, but they didn't come in the house. They just lived outside and helped catch field mice and snakes.

Mom had a small garden near the backdoor. Corn, wild berries, and tomatoes were planted yearly, and we ate much of our food from that garden. We had fresh eggs from our chickens, and Mom made all our bread from scratch. There would be a heavenly smell early in the morning as she would pull out the fresh-cooked bread from the oven. The aroma filled the house and made us want to wake up.

The iceman came once a week to bring a block of ice for the icebox. He carried large metal prongs that he used to pick up the ice block from the back of his truck. He would throw the ice to a leather shoulder pad so the cold and wet would stay off his clothes. He was very friendly, a happy man, and we were very happy to see him come and visit us.

One year at Christmastime, Mom let my older sisters take us to the courthouse for a Christmas party. It was the first time I saw Santa Claus. I was probably four years old, and I was scared of him, but he gave us toys and candy. Some other people came and sang songs and passed out candy canes.

The firemen from the fire station just down the road from us came to our house often to check on my mom. She would call them if she saw a snake in the yard, and they would come to kill the rattlesnakes and bring us some candy. They referred to my mom as the widow woman, and they just wanted to make sure that we were all right while living in this house without a dad. My older sisters and brothers went to school in Santa Monica. They would walk to the opening of Los Flores Canyon, and the school bus would pick them up. They left in the dark every morning and returned late in the afternoon. After my mom had to go on welfare to help support her family, the social worker helped Mom find a house in Santa Monica on Kensington Road. This house had three bedrooms and indoor plumbing. I spent most of my time in the bathroom those first days after moving in. I just loved the way the toilet flushed. The water just disappeared when you pushed the handle; "it was so great." The schools were all close, and my sisters and brother could walk to school and to catch the local bus to where they worked. Bounce moved with us, but all those cats just stayed behind. The chickens, well, they became Sunday dinner.

Las Flores Canyon Malibu home where Trudy and Lois were born,
Where Daddy died.   see Bouncy in driveway

In Malibu, in front of the Pippenberg house

Marge, Lois, Ellender, Trudy, Mimmie Pillars,
Joseph Pillars, Bounce, Lou, Doris, Nora, and Buck

Grandma Jones, Lou, Inez, Marge, Nora, and Ellender

Ellender's parents—Mimmie and Joseph Pillars
Malibu, California, 1942

Truman's parents—Elmer Rufus and Lily Bell Jones

Dad's brother, Uncle Emmett   Dad, Truman Jones

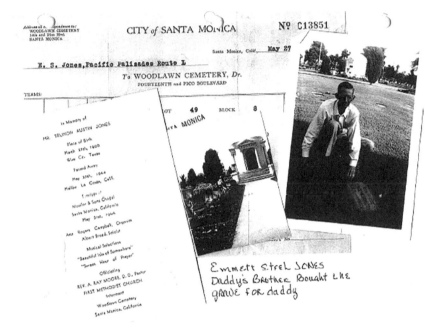

FILED JUL 12 1944 MAME B. BEATTY, County Recorder 6981

STATE OF CALIFORNIA
DEPARTMENT OF PUBLIC HEALTH   CERTIFICATE OF

This is a true certified copy of the record
if it bears the seal, imprinted in purple ink,
of the Registrar-Recorder.

FEE
$2.00 SEP 16 1975

REGISTRAR-RECORDER
LOS ANGELES COUNTY, CALIFORNIA

MARRIAGE LICENSE

STATE OF OKLAHOMA.

STEPHENS COUNTY

in County Court

TO ANY PERSON AUTHORIZED TO PERFORM AND SOLEMNIZE THE MARRIAGE CEREMONY—GREETING:

You are hereby authorized to join in marriage Mr. *Truman Jones* of *Duncan* County of *Stephens*, State of *Okla* aged *22* years, and M. *Ellender Peters*, of *Duncan* County of *Stephens*, State of *Okla*, aged *19* years.

And of this License you will make due return to my office within thirty days from this date,

Witness my hand and official seal, at **DUNCAN** in said County this *18* day of *Aug* A. D. 192*8*

_____ Court Clerk

By _____ Deputy

Recorded this *18* day of *Aug* 192*8*

_____ Court Clerk

By _____ Deputy

CERTIFICATE OF MARRIAGE

State of Oklahoma, **STEPHENS** County, ss.

I, *J. W. Quaid* Minister in *Methodist Protestant Church* of *Comanche*, in *Stephens* County, State of Oklahoma, do hereby certify that I joined in marriage the persons named in and authorized by this License to be married, on the *18th* day of *Aug.* A. D. 192*8*, at *Comanche*

Form 5

IT RECORD

1. FULL NAME ___Turmon Austin Jones___   DISTRICT No. __1974__   REGISTRAR'S No. __5__

2. PLACE OF DEATH: (A) COUNTY ___Los Angeles___
(B) CITY OR TOWN ___Santa Monica Rural___
IF OUTSIDE CITY OR TOWN LIMITS, WRITE RURAL
(C) NAME OF HOSPITAL OR INSTITUTION _____
___21237 Malibu LaCosta Rd.___
IF NOT IN HOSPITAL OR INSTITUTION, GIVE STREET NUMBER OR LOCATION

3. USUAL RESIDENCE OF DECEASED:
(A) STATE ___California___
(B) COUNTY ___Los Angeles___
(C) CITY OR TOWN ___Santa Monica Rural___
IF OUTSIDE CITY OR TOWN LIMITS, WRITE RURAL

LOS ANGELES COUNTY HEALTH DEPARTMENT

DIVISION OF VITAL RECORDS

CERTIFICATION

№ 111047

This is to certify that the attached is a full, true and correct copy of the

Certificate of _____ **Death** _____
(Birth - Death)

of _____ Turmon Austin Jones _____ which is
(Full Name)

on file in this office and of which I am legal custodian.

In testimony whereof, I have hereunto set my hand and affixed my seal

of office this ___29th___ day of ___December___, 19 __44__.

H. O. SWARTOUT, M.D., County Health Officer
and Registrar of Vital Statistics

Fee **$1.00**

By _____
Deputy Registrar of Vital Statistics

FD-VR7

DATE FILED   REGISTRAR'S SIGNATURE   ADDRESS ___Los Angeles___   May. 31, 44

STATE OF CALIFORNIA
DEPARTMENT OF PUBLIC HEALTH   **CERTIFICATE OF DEATH**   U. S. DEPT. OF COMMERCE
BUREAU OF THE CENSUS

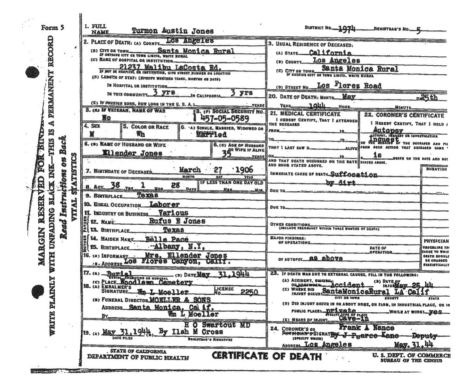

BEFORE THE INDUSTRIAL ACCIDENT COMMISSION OF THE STATE OF CALIFORNIA

CLAIM NO. L.A. 74-326

MRS. TRUMON JONES; and
MARJORIE JONES, IMA JO JONES,
ZELMA LOU JONES, ELEANORA
JONES, SCOTTY BUCK JONES,
DORIS FAYE JONES, LOIS MAYE
JONES and TRUDY ANGELA JONES,
minors, by their Guardian ad
Litem and Trustee, Mrs. Trumon
Jones,

　　　　　　　　　　　Applicants,

　　　　vs.

CHARLES PANTEL;
ARTHUR A. JONES, doing business as
Malibu Inn;
FRANK E. ALTOMARI, individually,
and FRANK E. ALTOMARI and R. L.
CURTIS, doing business as Malibu
La Costa Cafe;
AMERICAN AUTOMOBILE INSURANCE
COMPANY, a corporation; and
ROYAL INDEMNITY COMPANY,
a corporation,

　　　　　　　　　　　Defendants.

ORDER APPOINTING GUARDIAN AD
LITEM AND TRUSTEE, ORDER
APPROVING COMPROMISE AND
RELEASE, AND FINDINGS AND
ORDER

Mailed from San Francisco Office

JUN 8 - 1945

Industrial Accident Commission
State of California

GOOD CAUSE APPEARING THEREFOR:

IT IS ORDERED that Mrs. Trumon Jones be and she is hereby appointed Guardian ad Litem and Trustee for Marjorie Jones, Ima Jo Jones, Zelma Lou Jones, Eleanora Jones, Scotty Buck Jones, Doris Faye Jones, Lois Maye Jones and Trudy Angela Jones, minors, without bond.

　　　　　* * * * * * * * * * * *

The defendant, Charles Pantel, and the applicants in the above-entitled action filed their Compromise and Release, with request for its approval, on April 10, 1945, settling for $2,500.00.

This Commission, having now considered said Compromise and Release, as well as the entire record herein, finds that it should

Philip M. Schwabacher and Moe M. Fogel, applicants'
attorneys, are entitled to a lien for the reasonable value of their
services in the sum of $50.00, together with reimbursement in the
sum of $33.60 for necessary disbursements for depositions.

GOOD CAUSE APPEARING THEREFOR:

IT IS ORDERED that said Compromise and Release be and
it is hereby approved, payable to Mrs. Truman Jones, Trustee, for
the benefit of herself and said minors, at the rate of $10.00 per
week for 250 weeks beginning two weeks after date of service of this
Order.

IT IS FURTHER ORDERED that the defendant, Charles Fantel,
deduct the amounts heretofore allowed as liens and pay the same to
said attorneys at the rate of $5.00 per week, beginning two weeks
after date of service of this Order, until fully paid.

FINDINGS OF FACT

1. On May 25, 1944, the relationship of employer and
employee did not exist between the employee and Arthur A. Jones,
doing business as Malibu Inn; Frank E. Altomari, individually, and
Frank E. Altomari and R. L. Curtis, doing business as Malibu La
Costa Cafe.

2. Arthur A. Jones, doing business as Malibu Inn; Frank
E. Altomari, individually, and Frank E. Altomari and R. L. Curtis,
doing business as Malibu La Costa Cafe; American Automobile Insurance
Company, a corporation; and Royal Indemnity Company, a corporation,
are not proper parties defendant herein and are entitled to
dismissal herefrom.

L.A. 74-328   -2-

66

NOW, THEREFORE, IT IS ORDERED that Arthur G. Jones, doing business as Malibu Inn; Frank C. Altomari, individually, and Frank R. Altomari and R. L. Curtis, doing business as Malibu La Costa Cafe; American Automobile Insurance Company, a corporation; and Royal Indemnity Company, a corporation, be and they are hereby dismissed.

INDUSTRIAL ACCIDENT COMMISSION

PAUL SCHARRENBERG

A. WATCHMAN

Commissioners

Dated at San Francisco, California

JUN 1 - 1945

L.A. 74-380
FC:VR

CHAPTER 3

Moving to Santa Monica

California, 1948

Colorado Boulevard and the Sears store, Third Street Promenade, Pacific Palisades, Muscle Beach, Montana Avenue, Wilshire Boulevard, Santa Monica High School, Santa Monica Pier, Santa Monica City College, Santa Monica Beach—all these great places were a part of my life. I was beginning a journey, a new beginning, and none of these famous spots meant anything to me. I was only five years old.

In 1948, the Jones family moved to Santa Monica. Ellender Jones drove up in front of 714 Kensington Road. She drove an old Buick, all black and dusty. Inside that car were three little girls: Doris Faye (age six), Lois Maye (age five), and Trudy Angela (age four)—also a hinds-variety dog that we called Bouncy. Ellender drove up into a dirt driveway and looked at a house that she had just bought, a house that would be the new home for eight children: seven girls and one boy. Ellender opened the car door and just stood looking at this house. It was like a mansion to her. Never in her life had she believed that she would be able to afford a house of her own, a home in Santa Monica, California.

Truman Austin Jones was Ellender's husband and the father of her eight children, but he would not be joining us in Santa Monica because he died in Malibu on May 24, 1944. Mom was pregnant with Trudy when my dad died, so Mom needed help raising her eight children. With only an eighth grade education, it would be impossible for her to find work to support all her children, so she accepted state aid and was given a social worker to help her work out the finances.

Ellender had five hundred dollars in her savings account, and that was good enough for a down payment on a twelve-thousand-dollar house. With this house, she also got a vacant lot next to the house so she could have a garden. After all, she was just a farm girl. She knew how to plant flowers, vegetables, and fruit. She knew how to can all those food items, and she was ready that day to start digging in the ground.

Ellender told those three little girls that it was okay to get out of the car. She used her new key and opened the front door, and we were so excited to see a living room, dining room, kitchen, service porch, a fireplace, three bedrooms with closets, and what was this? Oh my, it was a bathroom, with running water and a toilet that flushed. At five years old, this was the first bathroom I had ever seen. In Malibu, we had an outhouse. It was up on the side of a hill, and we had to check for snakes before we could use it. At night, if we had to use the toilet, my mom would place a large bucket by the back door, and we used that. We never went to the outhouse after dark, too many creepy-crawly things moving around out there. But this toilet was inside the house. I stood and flushed that toilet for thirty minutes. I just loved watching the water come in and go down. It wasn't long before my older siblings started to come to this house from their school. They usually rode the bus from Santa Monica to Malibu; then they would walk up the canyon (Los Flores Canyon) to our house. Now they could just walk from their schools right to our new house.

Marge was in high school. Samohi, Lou, and Eleanor were at John Adams Junior High, and Buck was in grammar school. My sister Jo was living in Downey, California, at Rancho Los Amigos polio hospital. She had been there for several years, but we, the three little girls, were so young that we didn't get to go see her. You had to be eighteen to visit the polio hospital.

A moving truck came in the afternoon, and two men started moving in our things: three beds, a couple of dressers, a sofa, and a dining-room table. That was it. We were all home, spending the first night in our new house: Marge, Lou, and Eleanor in one bed; Doris, Lois, and Trudy in another. Mom was in her own bed, and Bucky slept on the sofa. Bounce slept in front of the fireplace.

The morning came fast. Everyone was using the bathroom, waiting for their turn to get ready for school. Mom was busy making lunches: peanut butter and jelly sandwich and a piece of fruit. They grabbed that lunch, and they were out the door. The social worker came that first morning. She sat with Mom and listed the money that Mom would receive for each child. Mom knew it would not be enough money to support the family, but she was so grateful, and she would work hard to make up the difference. I was hiding in the hallway while this new lady was there. I didn't like strangers. There was no way I was going to talk to her, so I just hid until she left.

The backyard was large. There were several large peach trees, a pomegranate tree, and a garage. There was a clothesline that hung from the house to one of the larger trees, and Mom said, "Good, now I can hang out clothes to dry on that line."

Soon we began exploring the neighborhood, just our street at first. Down on the corner, the corner of Lincoln and Kensington, there was a junkyard with a dirty old fence around it; it was a dirty, smelly place. On the other end of the street was a beautiful huge fenced-in yard. A very rich lady lived inside those big gates. We stood at the main gate and looked through the big iron gate, but we could only see a driveway and trees. Mom yelled at us, "You girls stay in our yard. Do not leave our house. We don't know anyone here yet. I don't want to have to go looking for you." We did as we were told.

I learned early in my new life that if you lived south of Santa Monica Boulevard, you were middle class; but if you lived south of Pico, then you were poor. We were definitely poor.

Mom worked hard ironing clothes for the neighbors and babysitting for the working families just to earn the smallest amount of money that was just enough for one more month. I never knew I was poor, never thought of that. I had food on the table, a place to sleep, friends to play with—I always felt safe. As long as my mom was there, I was happy.

We learned early that collecting pop bottles out of trash cans would get us money at the liquor store. We saved that change until three o'clock because the ice-cream truck would be coming down our street, and we could buy a popsicle for twenty-five cents.

As we grew older, we were able to take the number 3 bus on Lincoln Boulevard to the Venice Theater to see a movie or cartoon day, or go the other way into Santa Monica to the Criterion Theater to see Elvis's movie *Love Me Tender*, which was a real treat. We walked to the Fourth Street Park and watched the fireworks off the Santa Monica Pier. The beach was only seven blocks from our house. On Sunday afternoon, after church, we would take inner tubes from old tires, blow them up, and ride the wave in the Pacific Ocean. Sunburn? Oh yeah, we got so burned, and Mom would put canned milk on the burns so we could sleep at night. Sun protection, you ask? No such thing, and if there was, we couldn't afford it anyway.

When I was in the third grade, Deanna and Dolores Payne walked into my class at school. They were identical twins, and they were black girls, the first black students in our school or in our class. I knew instantly I wanted to be their friends. I was so happy when the teacher asked me if I would show them around the school. Yeahhhh! We were friends through junior high and high school. Deanna died in a car accident a few years after graduation. I still miss seeing her, and Dolores now lives in Berkeley, California.

First Day in Santa Monica Remembered

It was 1948, and I was five years old. Mom was driving her car. Trudy and me (Lois) and Bounce, our dog, were sitting in the backseat. The car smelled dusty and old, and the seat covers were wool and itchy, so I stood behind Mom, folding my arms across each other and laying my head on my arms. The car was full of things, and there wasn't much room for us to move around, but I can still remember that the seat covers made my legs itch, and they smelled very musty. It was a long ride to Santa Monica. I'm not sure that I knew where I was going, but it took a long time, and it was very hot in that car.

Doris and Bucky were riding in our Uncle Emmett's car with my uncle driving them, and his car was also full of household items for our new house.

When we arrived at the new house, I needed to use the outhouse, so Mom drove up at this new house on Kensington Street, and she told us to stay in the car, and she would go open the house's front door. When she said it was okay for us to get out of the car, I started looking around the back for an outhouse. I didn't know what an indoor bathroom was; I had never seen a house with indoor plumbing. I couldn't find that outhouse, and so I asked Lou, "Where is the outhouse?" She started laughing and said we didn't need an outhouse because we have a bathroom in the house now. She showed me where the bathroom was and said, "See? There is the toilet, and you can flush it." I was amazed. I flushed it several times just to watch the water swirl and go around and disappear through the bottom. This was the best part of this new house, a toilet that flushed, and I made sure that every new person who came in the house saw this toilet, and they had to watch the water swirl around and disappear in the bottom. They all laughed at me for days. I still remember that it was discussed at the Sunday dinner, and everyone had a great laugh. I still think it was great.

The three girls each went to bed while Buck slept on the sofa. Mom chopped wood for the fireplace. Marge, Lou, and Nora got to go to school. I didn't want to go to school, no way. I was shy and afraid of everyone. I hid in the closet a few times when the neighbors came to visit, especially a man. They looked scary to me; I only liked my brother. My first day of school was a nightmare. I am now seventy-one years old, and I can remember it like it was yesterday.

Doris was one year older. She had been in kindergarten already, so Mom told her to walk me to school on my first day. It was just two blocks from our house, down our street, down the alley, and there was John Muir School. Doris took me to this room and said she would be back later. I started to cry. The teacher was Mrs. Mathis. She tried to get me to stop crying by showing me this room, but I just wanted to go home. It seemed like forever, crying in the corner. This little girl came over and sat next to me. She was blonde, tiny, and had fair skin. She said, "If you stop crying, I will be your friend" We did become friends, and she is my dearest friend to this very day. Her name is Michele Rivard, and we have been friends for sixty-six years. Each day, she would meet me by the door of the classroom, and she would take my hand, and we would go into the room together. Mrs. Mathis let us always sit together. I am sure it was the only way I would not start crying again.

I was the ninth child of Ellender and Truman Jones. My father died when I was only one year old, so unfortunately, I never knew him. I had the good fortune to have a lot of sisters and one brother, and I remember that my sisters would be around to protect me. I felt left out of all the family decisions. Mom would say, "Shhhh, watch your mouth. Little ears are listening." There was a lot of whispering going on in the house. I always felt afraid and insecure. I was terrified of going to spend the night at someone else's house. I don't know where I got this mind-set, but I always felt that Mom would die, and we would be left all alone. I loved this big family and was happy to be a part of it. I never thought we were poor, and I didn't know what welfare meant. I just knew that some lady was coming, and she didn't like children, so we had to leave. I was in junior high school before I realized that this welfare lady would take Mom's check away if she saw her receiving money for babysitting the neighbors' children.

I had a great childhood. I always had someone to play with. I had two close friends who lived next door: Carol and Linda Foley. They had great dolls, storybook dolls, and liked to hopscotch and jump-rope with me. Norma Tipper lived across the street, and she had only a mom who worked all day. Norma would stay alone, so she spent a lot of time at our house. They lived in a one-bedroom apartment, and I felt bad for her that she didn't have any brothers and sisters. My mom stayed home all day, and we always had visitors. What could be better than this?

It was later in about the seventh grade that my life changed. All the popular girls at John Adams Junior High were having their first friends party, and I wanted to go so had. More than anything, I wanted an invitation to their house, but I wasn't invited, so I asked my friend Michele why I didn't get an invitation. She said, "Because you are poor." I was so surprised she said that. She said, "Those girls said that your clothes are old-looking and your shoes have holes in them." Whatever self-esteem I had, it was now gone. I became very shy, stayed to myself, and only had Michele for my friend. I would not raise my hand in class, wouldn't answer any questions, and I always sat in the back of the classroom. One day, I asked my mom, "What does welfare mean? Does it mean I am poor?" She said, "Do you feel poor?" I said, "No." Then she said, "Just do your homework and don't worry about it." As I look back on those days, those years, it amazes me to this day that just one conversation changed the course of my life for the next six years.

Why Santa Monica

Marge, Lou, and Nora were already in schools in Santa Monica. The social worker told my mom that it was impossible to bus seven children to Santa Monica every day. It would also be easier for Mom to get a job in the city rather than in a rural area as Malibu. Mom had a five-hundred-dollar savings. That was all the money she had, so the social worker told her that they could find a house in Santa Monica close to the schools, close to the bus line, close to a church, and close to shopping. When they found the Kensington house, it also had a lot next door to the property, and Mom could purchase both pieces, the house and lot, for twelve thousand dollars.

That was more money than she could possibly afford, but if the older girls, Marge and Lou, could get jobs after school, plus the welfare money, they could swing the purchase of the properties, and that was what Mom did. The girls did find jobs. Mom could not leave the four youngest children alone, so she started ironing neighbors' clothes, grew vegetables in the lot next to the house, and babysat whenever she was needed—and they just barely skimmed by each month.

Mom had considered to move to Downey to be closer to Jo in Rancho Los Amigos Hospital, but the doctors had told Mom that Jo would probably not live, so at the time, Santa Monica was her best choice.

Mom read her Bible and prayed every day for her needs, for her children to stay healthy. She worked long hours, and God blessed her.

John Muir Grammar School was only two blocks from our house, with an easy access through the alley. John Adams Junior High was just seven blocks away, and Santa Monica High School only five block away, so we could all walk to school easily. This was a huge plus in the planning process.

Though we were poor and I didn't know what welfare meant, I just knew that some lady was coming, and she didn't like children, so we had to leave. I was in junior high school before I realized that this welfare lady would take Mom's check away if she saw her receiving money for babysitting the neighbors' children.

Bounce

He never had a collar, leash, or license. He just always hung around, and he adopted our family in the mid-'40s. He just showed up one day, and Mom said he could stay. We always felt like he was Buck's dog, but he belonged to all of us, and we all treated this dog like family.

When we moved from Malibu to Santa Monica, I can remember getting into the car. We were all packed and ready to drive to our new house when someone said, "Where is Bounce? Bouncy, Bouncy, where are you?" Suddenly the dog showed up, got into the car with us, and off we went to live in Santa Monica.

This dog had such a free spirit about him. He ate scraps from our table because Mom never bought dog food. She would never have thought to give him rabies vaccination or vitamins—what! This was a dog, after all. Bounce would eat at night and usually be gone all day; he just roamed the streets between Lincoln Boulevard and the Santa Monica Beach. He liked going to the ocean each day and swimming in the water. He never had fleas that we noticed; it must have been the saltwater that killed them. He raided trash cans and ran after cats, but no one cared where he went or when he might return; he just always did. Usually around dinnertime, he would come walking slowly into the yard, eat, and sleep by the fireplace in our front room.

Bounce never chased a ball, and I can't remember him doing any tricks. He was just there, a member of the family. We all loved him, especially Buck. Mom would sometimes refer to him as that "dang dog," especially if he knocked over the trash or jumped at the clothes hanging on the line to dry. If the wind would blow just the right way, Bounce could jump just high enough to catch a piece of the cloth, and down it would come. Once the piece of clothing was on the ground, he could have cared less. It was chasing the wind that got him excited.

I was in my late teens when Bounce died. He came, stayed, and lived with us; and then one day, he was just gone. Mom found him out back, curled up next to pomegranate tree. When I think about this wonderful pet, I just smile that he had a perfect life— never chained up, never forced to walk a certain path, never kept behind gates or a fence. He came when he wanted to; he left when he wanted to. He always had food to eat, always had a warm fireplace to sleep next to, and he had a family that loved him. Perfect! What more could a dog want?

Ellender Has a Dream

After Truman died and Ellender was left with eight children to raise, she wondered if she would be able to take care of all these children. How would she feed them? The relatives started coming around, suggesting to her that the children should be split up, and maybe some of Truman's sisters could adopt one or two children just to make life a little easier for Ellender. Fortunately for all eight of her children, she wasn't about to get rid of any of them.

She was going to stand firm and find a way to raise her children even if she had to do it all by herself.

I am the ninth child. I don't remember my dad because I was only one year and two months when he died. We lived in Malibu, California, in a rented house that was lovingly called the Pippenberg house. I was born in this house in 1943. My mom cleaned houses, and with help from her parents, she was able to stay in this house until I was five years old. The social worker helped Mom find a house in Santa Monica, and we moved there when I was five years old in 1948.

When I was about the age of ten, I remember hearing my mom say things like, "I sure hope all my girls find a good man to take care of them." My sister Marge was thirteen years older than me, so by this time, she had met Jack La Vancil and was married. My sister Lou was married to George Donoho, and I remember thinking, *I don't want to get married to some old man.* Twenty years old seemed old to me.

As I got older, I would hear Mom saying to friends or neighbors, "I just want to get my girls all married to good men. Girls need to be married and have children of their own, be good cooks, and keep those men happy." Now, about this same time, my brother was three years older than me. Mom never said he should get married; in fact, it was just the reverse. My brother loved to go to the Santa Monica Pier and be around all the men down there. He wanted to learn how to fish and drive a boat. All he thought about was getting through school and getting a job down at that pier. Mom would say, "Buck just needs to be around those men down there. I don't mind as long as he graduates from high school."

RECORDING REQUESTED BY   1136   BKR2293PG770

when recorded mail to

Mrs. Ellender Jones

714 Kensington Road

Santa Monica, California

RECORDED IN OFFICIAL RECORDS
OF LOS ANGELES COUNTY, CALIF.
FOR TITLE INSURANCE & TRUST CO.

JUN 21   1965 AT 8 A.M.

RAY E. LEE, County Recorder

COUNTY OF LOS ANGELES   space above this line for recorder's use   DEPARTMENT OF CHARITIES

SATISFACTION AND DISCHARGE OF MORTGAGE

KNOW ALL MEN BY THESE PRESENTS:

That the County of Los Angeles, State of California, MORTGAGEE, for a valuable consideration, does hereby certify and declare that a certain mortgage bearing date the 8th day of October, 19 60, made and executed by ELLENDER JONES, a widow, MORTGAGOR, to County of Los Angeles, MORTGAGEE, and recorded in Book T 1648, Page 848, Official Records of Los Angeles County, and that certain mortgage bearing the date the 14th day of November, 1960, made and executed by ELLENDER JONES, a widow

MORTGAGORS, to County of Los Angeles, MORTGAGEE, and recorded in Book T 1677 Page 879, Official Records of Los Angeles County, State of California, has been fully SATISFIED, PAID and DISCHARGED.

IN WITNESS WHEREOF, the said County has, by order of its Board of Supervisors, caused these presents to be executed in its name by the Superintendent of Charities, or an Officer designated by him and attested by the Clerk thereof, this 17th day of JUNE, 19 65.

COUNTY OF LOS ANGELES
BY WILLIAM A. BARR
SUPERINTENDENT OF CHARITIES

ATTEST:

By *Aaron Lohr*

An Officer designated to execute
said Instrument

WILLIAM G. SHARP, County Clerk of the County
of Los Angeles, State of California

By *Marian A. Lotora*

Deputy

COUNTY OF LOS ANGELES } ss
STATE OF CALIFORNIA }

On this 17th day of JUNE, 1965, before me, WILLIAM G. SHARP, County Clerk of the County of Los Angeles, State of California, and Clerk of the Superior Court in and for said County and State, personally appeared AARON LOHR known to me to be an Officer designated by the Superintendent of Charities of the County that executed the within instrument to execute the within instrument and the person who executed the within instrument on behalf of the County therein named and acknowledged to me that said County executed the same.

Santa Monica,   California

──────── space above this line for recorder's use ────────

COUNTY OF LOS ANGELES   DEPARTMENT OF CHARITIES

SATISFACTION AND DISCHARGE OF MORTGAGE

KNOW ALL MEN BY THESE PRESENTS:

That the County of Los Angeles, State of California, MORTGAGEE, for a valuable consideration, does hereby certify and declare that a certain mortgage bearing date the 8th   day of October , 19 60 , made and executed by ELLENDER JONES, a widow, MORTGAGOR, to County of Los Angeles, MORTGAGEE, and recorded in Book T 1648, Page 848, Official Records of Los Angeles County, and that certain mortgage bearing the date the 14th day of November, 1960, made and executed by ELLENDER JONES, a widow

MORTGAGORS, to County of Los Angeles, MORTGAGEE, and recorded in Book T 1677 Page 879   , Official Records of Los Angeles County, State of California, has been fully SATIS-FIED, PAID and DISCHARGED.

IN WITNESS WHEREOF, the said County has, by order of its Board of Supervisors, caused these presents to be executed in its name by the Superintendent of Charities, or an Officer designated by him and attested by the Clerk thereof, this 17th   day of   JUNE   , 19 65 .

COUNTY OF LOS ANGELES
BY WILLIAM A. BARR
SUPERINTENDENT OF CHARITIES

ATTEST:

WILLIAM G. SHARP, County Clerk of the County of Los Angeles, State of California

By *Marcia A. Lotora*

Deputy

By *Aaron Lohr*

An Officer designated to execute said Instrument

COUNTY OF LOS ANGELES } ss
STATE OF CALIFORNIA }

On this   17th   day of   JUNE   , 19 65 , before me, WILLIAM G. SHARP, County Clerk of the County of Los Angeles, State of California, and Clerk of the Superior Court in and for said County and State, personally appeared   AARON LOHR known to me to be an Officer designated by the Superintendent of Charities of the County that execut-ed the within instrument to execute the within instrument and the person who executed the within in-strument on behalf of the County therein named and acknowledged to me that said County executed the same.

IN WITNESS WHEREOF, I have hereunto set my hand and affixed my official seal the day and year in this certificate first above written.

WILLIAM G. SHARP, County Clerk and Clerk of the said Superior Court of the State of California for the County of Los Angeles

By *Marcia A. Lotora*

Deputy

T6R140—MA T80-1—4/64

1136

84

CHAPTER 4

Ima Jo Comes Home

Breakfast was cold cereal and homemade bread sliced for toast. We always ate fast on Saturday mornings. This was the day that we get to play our side with our friends. Most mornings, we woke up early, cleaned our room, and got ready for school. Mom would be at the ironing board already; she always got an early start. She was ironing someone else's clothes—for the neighbors, for friends, for church families. She ironed every day to make extra money for our family. Before our breakfast was over, there was a knock at the door. It was Carol and Linda, our neighbors and friends. Mom answered the door. Carol said, "Can Lois and Trudy come out to play?" "Okay," said Mom, "but stay close to the house."

We decided to play hopscotch. We all loved this game, and I was really good at it. We didn't have a real good marker, so we used three bobby pins clipped together. Carol had a great lager. She had a rabbit's foot hooked to a chain; now she was very lucky. We used the out in the front of our house because it was flat there. We found a piece of green chalk; it was perfect to mark the squares so we can begin our game.

Now, if you don't know the game of hopscotch, it is blocks drawn on the concrete: first one then two blocks next to each other, then one again for four, right up to the number ten. The idea is to throw the lager into the square then jump on one foot to each square up to ten, turn around, come back, and pick up your marker without touching the second foot on the ground, so simple, but you needed really good balance. Now, if you step on a line or touch your second foot to the ground, your turn is over, and the next in line begins their turn.

Our world was small. We were children who were very content to play, and little did we know that on this Saturday, something very important was going to happen, something that would change the Jones family forever. Six girls and one boy and Mom, this was our family. Trudy was the youngest at five years old; I was next at six (I am Lois). Doris was third (she was seven), and we were known as the three little girls.

Mom called us this because the next person in line was a boy: my brother, Scotty Buck, better known to us as Bucky. He was nine. Eleanor was eleven; we called her Nora. Zelma Lou was next, known only as Lou; she was thirteen. And my oldest sister was Marjorie Lucile, and we called her Marge or Mert. She was in high school and was seventeen.

The social worker who was assigned to Mom worked with her to find the right house for our family, somewhere close to schools, markets, the bus line, and businesses that could provide my older sisters with jobs. We were a close family. We all cared about one another, and we were happy.

Mom yelled out the front door, "You kids stay clean. We're having company soon." We continued with our hopscotch game. Life was good.

Then our world changed. This big white car came to a stop in front of our house. It was really long and had windows down the side of it. Two red lights were flashing over the front window. Two men got out. They were wearing white shirts, white pants, and white shoes. They walked to the back of the car and opened a large back door. Our game stopped. No one said a word; we just stood there and stared at this amazing thing that was happening. The men pulled out a long bed with a girl strapped down to it. I looked at her. She was so beautiful; she was smiling at us. Trudy ran to the house and yelled for Mom, but as I turned to the house, I saw Mom standing on the porch. She was crying. Marge had her arms around Mom's shoulders, and she was also crying. Betty was Carol and Linda's mother. I saw her coming, walking fast across her lawn, across our driveway, and up the front steps. Betty gave Mom a big hug; she was all smiles. The men took the girl into the house and lifted her onto a bed, a large white bed, which I later discovered was from the hospital.

Who was this person? Why was Mom crying? We had so many questions. The bed was pushed over in front of a big window so this girl could see outside to the yard.

Everyone was so busy getting things moved around. Mom was hugging this girl, Marge was hugging this girl, and Trudy and I were just staring. This new girl had the longest hair that I had ever seen. It flowed from the top of her head across her shoulders, down her back, and up over her bottom. Her hair was dark brown, shiny, and everyone was touching her long braids. I whispered to Mom, "Who is she?" Mom said, "Who is she? She is your sister Jo. She has come home from the hospital, and she is going to live with us now." Until that very moment, I didn't remember anyone ever talking about her. I probably did. We had pictures of her with us at the Malibu house, but I had forgotten her. She had been gone for more than five years, and I was only six years old.

This was great! Another sister and a big chair with wheels on it. Could we sit in it? Could we push one another around the house in it? This was going to be a lot of fun. Lou and Marge told us later in the day that Jo had polio, and she was not able to walk; that was why she had a special chair, so that she could move around. Marge said, "Jo is never going to walk, and this special chair will help support her back and her legs." I didn't care that she had polio. This was great. I could show her off to my friends. She was like a new toy.

I really liked bringing friends over to say hi to her. Jo would wave at them, and they would smile at her and then run away. I liked the nights best. After our bath, I would sit next to Jo's bed with my head up against her mattress, and Jo would brush my hair. She would tell us stories about her friends at the hospital. She would tell us about our daddy and how he used to come to the hospital to see her. He would bring candy for all the polio kids on her floor, she said.

He would sing songs to her and give her a lot of kisses. No one talked about our daddy very much. I guess it was just too hard, too painful.

I hated going to school. We only lived two blocks from John Muir Grammar School. I was in kindergarten. I had to walk the two blocks to school and back home by myself; I was so afraid. When I told Jo about this, she said, "You don't have to be afraid because every day, when you come home, the first thing you're going to see is me smiling at you through this window. I will always be here for you." I truly believe this conversation was the only reason I made it through to the sixth grade, just knowing that Jo was waiting for me to come home.

Marge had a boyfriend named Jack. He came over a lot. We all liked him very much. He made Mom laugh, and he brought us candy. He had a fancy car, and he would pick Jo up, put her in the car with him and Marge, and they would go to the drive-in theater. They would go to church together and to parties. The three little girls couldn't wait to grow up so we could go with them.

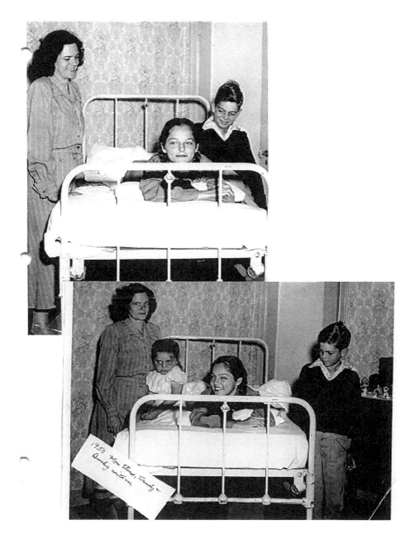

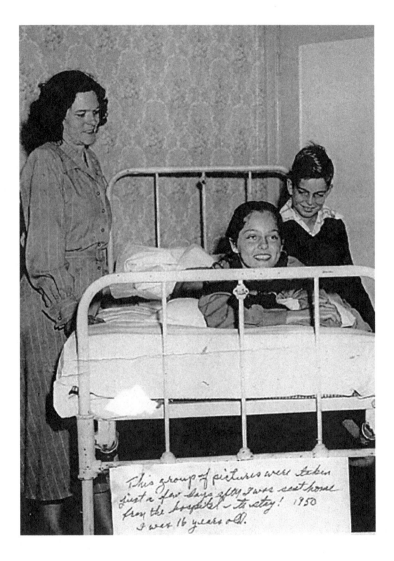

This group of pictures were taken just a few days after I was sent home from the hospital – to stay! 1950 I was 16 years old.

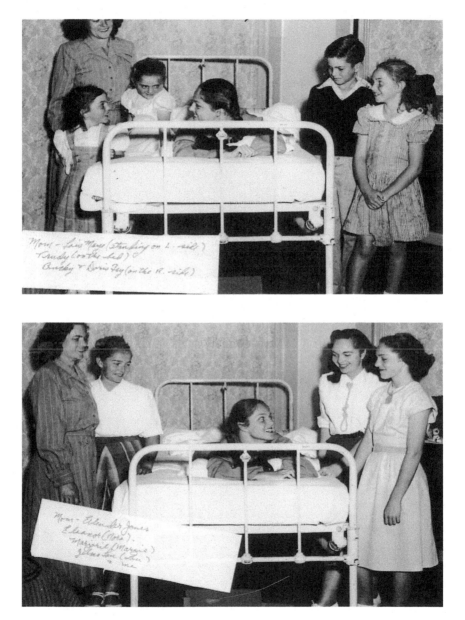

Ima Jo: The Early 1950

This was an amazing time for our family. Jo being home with us was only the beginning of an amazing journey. Jo's home teacher, Mrs. Deichman, came three times a week; and even though Jo had no formal education up to this point, Mrs. Deichman told Mom that Jo was very bright and was learning very quickly.

We had a good relationship with our neighbors. We had friends to play with; and my sisters Marge, Lou, and Nora all had jobs after school. We also had found a good church to go to. In three short years, Jo completed high school and graduated with the Santa Monica High school graduating class, but she didn't know anyone at the school. She had all her classes at home with Mrs. Deichman. Mom made a cake, and we had a party. Lots of friends from church came. We didn't have a lot of parties, so this was a special time for all of us.

Mom had a meeting with the state social worker, and there was good news for sure: Jo would be able to attend Santa Monica City College. The state would provide a driver (Bob Woods) who would pick Jo up every day and take her to all her classes and bring her home. Jo loved college. She made friends very quickly, and the teachers made every accommodation for her wheelchair. She attended all the football games, and she liked the girls' volleyball team. Even though she couldn't participate in any sports activity, she was there to cheer on her friends. Jo's grades were outstanding, and she was on the dean's list for exceptional scholastic achievement.

In 1956, Jo won the Santa Monica City College Campus Sweetheart award—Miss Spin-Drift 1956. One year later, she graduated with honors and was given the greatest gift that anyone could imagine for Jo. Because of her accomplishments, the State Department of Social Work gave Jo a scholarship to a university of her choice. She chose Riverside Baptist College; this was her dream. Mom was worried that she wouldn't be able to manage away from home because someone had to get her out of bed, dress her, help her get to the dining room for breakfast, and get to her classes. No problem! A lady named Lucky Buchay came into the picture. Lucky was a big girl, extremely capable of caring for Jo and could handle any problem. She said she would take care of all Jo's special needs, and so the college gave Lucky a full scholarship to the college also. Without the scholarship, she would not be able to attend college.

At Riverside Baptist College, Jo met Tom Gorrell. Tom was studying to be a minister. Jo and Tom fell in love, and against so many doubts, they were married, had three children, and lived in Denver, Colorado. In 1999, at the age of sixty-five, Jo died from polio complications. She and Tom had seven grandchildren.

Many stories of courage, laughter, sorrow, fear came into play for our family through these many years. My mom died in October 1998, one year before Jo.

Miss Spin-Drift

It was 1956. Jo had completed her high school requirements. She graduated from Santa Monica High School, received her diploma, but never attended Samohi, not even one day. Mrs. Deichman had been her home teacher for three years; she was a lady of rigid rules. "Study hard," she would tell Jo. "You have many years to catch up on." She would come early in the morning and sit next to Jo's hospital bed, and together, they worked on her lessons.

Now that Jo had completed her high school requirements, what was she supposed to do? Mrs. Deichman did not teach college. She worked for the State of California in the handicapped children home study program, and now her work was done. Mom worried about Jo and how she would allow her to continue her education. Most people thought Jo could become a teacher. She was very smart—a quick study, they called it. What would she do with the rest of her life? How would she make money to survive on her own? Was any of this possible? Mom shed many tears about what would happen if she died. Who would take care of Jo?

Finally, the answer came. A teacher from Santa Monica City College heard of Jo's dilemma. She suggested that the state might pay for a care person for Jo, someone who could lift her into a car, lift her into her wheelchair without hurting her, take her to her classes, and get her home each day. Mom talked to our social worker about this program, and the social worker began working on the possibility. The answer finally came. There was a young man who lived just a couple of blocks from our house who had signed up for school at the college and was looking for a job. His name had been placed on the college bulletin board. They contacted Bob Woods, and he came to our house to meet Mom and Jo. After mom told him about Jo's body, how careful he needed to be with her, and the responsibility involved, he agreed, as did Jo, and everyone started signing papers.

Late in the summer, the mail came from the State of California disability department. The program had been accepted, and Jo could start at SMCC in the fall. Our family was thrilled. Mom held a prayer meeting at the house, and she served cake and ice cream for the celebration.

The entire neighborhood of friends and family were outside waiting for Bob to arrive. I think she was very surprised that so many people cared about this event. Mom had already put Jo into her wheelchair, helped her to get dressed, and given her a new notebook, pen, pencil, and a small lunch. Jo was waiting in the entrance to the front door. She was all smiles when she saw Bob arrive. He smiled back, pushed the wheelchair to his car, and carefully, very carefully (everyone was watching him), lifted her into the car. Bob was very strong. He lifted her like she weighed a feather. He said, "Are you okay?" She said, "Yes, I am fine." He got into the driver's seat, and off they went. Mom turned and went into the house. We all knew that she was very nervous, but like any parent who loves and protects their children, she needed to let go.

Jo attended college five days a week, and she would study all weekend, of course taking time to go to church on Sunday morning with the entire family.

Dinnertime was a big occasion at our house. Everyone was gone during the day, either working or going to school, so it was during the evening meal that we got to see one another. Mom made simple meals, but they were so good. And sometimes, to this very day in 2008, I just think about a meal that Mom had cooked, and I can still taste the sweetness of red beans, ham hocks, corn bread, lots of butter, and a glass of milk. Yes, we crumbled our corn bread into our milk, stirred it up, and made like a mash out of it. No one else would think to do such a thing, but Mom had done it when she lived on the farm; and if it was good enough for her, then it's okay with us.

This particular dinner was a little different, and it was because Jo was sitting at the table with us. Mom had moved the chairs around and pulled Jo's chair right up to the table. Usually, Jo would eat in her bed. Mom would make a plate for her and serve it to her in her room. It was a bedroom in front of the house. It had a big window right by Jo's bed so she could see out and wave to people going about their daily lives. This was the room where we all liked to gather in because this was where Jo was, but not today. Jo was having dinner with us. We were sharing the day we had, and Jo said, "I have some good news." We all stopped and looked at her. "Today I was nominated for Miss Spin-Drift." We just stared because none knew what she was talking about. "What is that?" someone asked. "Well," Jo said, "it's the homecoming queen. Every year, at the end of the school year, the football team has a big championship game, and they choose a girl from the class to be the homecoming queen. They get to ride on a float, like the rose parade, and then they have a big dance after."

It was dead silence. "But, Jo, you can't dance!" "Well, that's true, but it is nice to be nominated. They have three other gals. They're all so beautiful, the cheerleaders, the class president. You know, real popular girls, so I don't think I will be chosen. But I get my picture in the school newspaper." Wow, the school newspaper. For our family, this was a great thing, and we all were so happy for Jo that this could happen for her. No one in our family ever had their name or picture in the newspaper. I believe it was about three weeks before this queen would be chosen. Jo didn't say much about it, but we wanted to see Jo's picture with the other three chosen nominees in the school newspaper. Maybe, just maybe, it would be in the *Evening Outlook*, our local Santa Monica paper.

It was on a Wednesday, just before the big football game, with the homecoming game to be played on Friday night. Bob came to pick Jo up in the morning, nothing out of the ordinary. We all went about our business as usual, and then Bob brought Jo home, but they were not alone. There was a lot of noise, horns honking, people yelling out of their cars. I've never heard such a loud noise on our street. Of course, we all ran to the front door to see what was happening. Jo was smiling and laughing. She was holding the newspaper and saying, "Mom, I won! I won, Mom! I am Miss Spin-Drift for the homecoming game! Look, Mom, my picture is on the front page." We all jumped for joy. Mom was crying. Praise God for such a wonderful gift to our family, for Jo, just a little crippled girl who got a break in life.

"Mom, I need a formal. The queen needs a formal, and I get to ride on the float. They are going to fix my wheels to the floor of the float so that I can't roll off. And, Mom, I get to wear a crown."

Mom and Marge went shopping for a formal for Jo. Mom didn't have much money, but she heard they were having a sale at Learner in Santa Monica on Third Street. So off they went. They found the perfect dress, and Mom was telling the saleslady about the great event that would take place in just two days. The saleslady said, "Would you accept the dress as a gift from me? I would love to be a part of this." Mom couldn't believe how much everyone was trying to be so helpful, so excited. This was bigger than any wedding we had ever seen.

Friday evening came, and we all got to go to the football game. The game was okay, but when halftime started, everyone was on their feet. The band began to play as they marched across the field, and now here came the parade. A convertible carried the third runner-up, the second car carried the second runner-up, and the convertible carried the first runner-up. And then, like a beautiful chariot, a long white float appeared, and there was Jo in her wheelchair, flowers everywhere. She was wearing a purple cape with white fur trim and a diamond tiara on her head. Everyone was cheering, everyone was standing, and Jo was smiling and waving to the crowd. She was stunning, glorious beyond words. The float came to a stop right in front of the grandstand, and the football team came running across the field and gathered all around Jo. They were clapping and cheering for her. The float began to move again. The team returned to their side of the field, and we didn't see Jo again until the next morning. She had come in sometime during the night; Bob brought her home from the dance very late. We were all asleep, and Mom put Jo to her bed. She was still wearing the tiara. She said to Mom, "I had a great time tonight, Mom. I danced every dance." The guys lined up, placed their hands on the front of her chair, and swished her all over the dance floor. She said, "Mom, I got dizzy, but I loved every minute of it."

It made our family so happy to know that so many people loved Jo. She had a contagious smile and just wanted to be a friend to everyone. She had great grades, and she was an inspiration to so many people in Santa Monica City College. The last month of school came to an end. Jo graduated from Santa Monica City College. Now what? What did life have in store for her now? We were only thinking about going to the beach, playing with our friends, and Jo sat in the window and watched everyone at play.

Miss Spin-Drift Of 1956

Jo's Big Announcement (1957)

My eight grade was pretty much a blur. I don't remember a lot about this particular year for me. I must have been about fourteen years old, going to school at John Adams Junior High in Santa Monica. My day began the same each day: get up, make my bed, dress, eat breakfast, and go to school. I walked to and from school each day. It seemed like a long way at the time, but now, when I see the street that I walked on, it wasn't so bad, from Lincoln Boulevard up Pearl Street to Sixteenth Street. Lincoln was considered the Seventh Street, so it was nine blocks to school each day, each way, of course.

Now, in the midst of this routine each day, something exciting was going to happen. My sister Jo was going to Riverside Baptist College, better known as California Baptist University. It was a four-hour drive to Riverside from Santa Monica. There were very few freeways in those days. We had to drive through Los Angeles, Pomona, and Corona, and then into Riverside. I just knew it took forever to get there.

Today Mom received a phone call from Jo. She said, "Mom, I am coming home this weekend, and I am bringing a friend with me, a guy friend." Jo couldn't drive, and her roommate, Lucky, was not coming, so who was this guy she wanted us to meet? Why was this guy driving her home? We couldn't wait till Saturday to see Jo. It had been several months since she was able to come home, so this was going to be a great day. Everyone in the house was busy cleaning. Mom put away her ironing board. Now, she never put away that ironing board for anyone, so what was going on?

Mom shoved everything into a closet in the hallway. The house needed to be especially clean for this guest.

A car drove up into the driveway. We were all running to the front door like crazy people, you would have thought Jesus was coming; we were so excited. Jo received hugs from everyone in the house: five girls, one boy, and of course, Mom. Betty Foley, our neighbor, was there also. She was always at our house when something special was about to happen.

Tom Gorrell stood to the side of the car, just watching all of us crazy family members getting so excited. He was very good-looking, just smiling and not saying a word. Tom looked very nervous. Maybe he wasn't prepared for so many people when he arrived. Mom walked over to him and said, "Hello, I'm Jonesy, Jo's mother. Thank you for driving her home." Jo said, "Mom, this is Tom Gorrell, my friend from college." Mom said, "Nice to meet you, Tom. Come on into the house."

We all gathered in the living room to talk, and Mom wanted to know if everything was good at school: "How are your grades?"

"How is your roommate, Lucky?" "Have you been getting enough sleep?" Jo told mom that everything was going well. Her grades were really good, and she loved living at the college, and she had a job in the front office. This job helped pay for her room and board.

It was now very quiet in the room. Jo said, "Mom, Tom and I want to get married." There was dead silence. Then Mom said, "Whaaaaat? Did you say married? For heaven sakes, Jo, you can't get married. You can't cook or clean house. Who is going to help you get dressed? You can't sit on the toilet like a normal person. Who will help you with your bedpan (just like the ones used in a hospital)?" Tom said, "Mrs. Jones, I will do all those things for Jo. I love her. God brought us together. We want to get married." Mom said, "Well, when Jo finishes school, then we'll talk about it again." "No!" said Tom. "We want to get married now. You see, I've been called into the air force, and I have to report for duty in just a few weeks in Texas. I want to take Jo with me."

"For land's sake, we can't be ready by then, so much to do. What will our friends at the church say?" Mom was very right with this question. Our church was our family. We did everything at the church. It was our life, and they were stunned when Jo just wanted to go to Riverside and attend college. Getting married was out of the question.

The first person Mom called on the phone was our pastor. He said, "No! Jo can't have children or care for herself. This is a crazy idea. Tom has no idea what he is in for. They need serious counseling, Jonesy. No way will I marry these kids. What if he leaves her strained somewhere? And he will want a divorce." No one in our family had gotten a divorce; this was so upsetting to Mom. The phone didn't stop ringing. Everyone told Mom to say no. "Jo can't have children, can't cook, can't take care of herself." The answer was simple: just say no.

Tom stayed the night, and he did go to church with the family on Sunday. I remember everyone starring at us, all of us, when we walked into the sanctuary. I hated everyone staring. What was the matter with these people?

On Monday, Mom called our family doctor and asked if Jo and Tom could come and speak with him. It was easy to see our family physician. Mom knew him well with all these kids, and many times, he came to our house to help someone who was sick. Yes, this was a time when doctors made house calls.

Jo and Tom met him in his office, and they told him that they wanted to get married. He said to them, "Children are out of the question for you. It cannot happen." He also said they should not adopt because it was unreasonable for anyone to think Jo could care for a child when she couldn't care for herself. They came back to the house so disappointed. Tom said, "I don't care what he said, Jo, and I want to be married. We have discussed every problem that might come up, and we don't care. We will work it out ourselves. We can do this." Tom continued to say, "She's going to do fine. I will teach her to cook. We will clean together. She will stay on base with me so that I can get to her quickly and put her into bed when she needs to lie down. Mrs. Jones, Jo and I are going to get married, and we want your blessing." Mom began to cry. "Okay," she said. "No time for me to make a dress. We'll have to buy one."

Tuesday morning, Tom and Jo left and returned to Riverside. They wanted to finish the last semester, just two weeks to go. They would not stay and graduate. When they returned to Santa Monica in just three short weeks, preparation started for this church wedding. There was no time for invitations. An announcement was given at church that everyone was invited. Phone calls were made to family and friends, and the neighbors were all invited by Mom. The ladies of the church said they would decorate the church basement for a large reception area. Cake and punch would be served; there were no sit-down lunches or dinners in those days. The most expensive part of this would be the girls' bridesmaid dresses. Jo's wedding dress and Tom's military uniform was brought in from Texas by a friend.

Lou and Nora were bridesmaids, and David Short, six years old, was ring bearer. Pastor Ferguson refused to do the ceremony; he said they were making a big mistake. Marge called her pastor, Charles Clinard. He said he would be honored.

The church was packed with people, and there was standing room only in the back. My brother, Buck, pushed Jo down the aisle. Her wedding dress was so beautiful and hung to the floor all around the front of her wheelchair. Her bouquet was a gift from her roommate, Lucky. For so much organization, so much hurry all week, everything was ready. Pastor announced them as husband and wife. Everyone cheered; a great applause could be heard throughout the building. Jo was all smiles; she was so happy. As they left the church, Tom's military buddies had crossed swords for them to pass under—wow, what an exciting day. What I didn't know was when they drove away from the church, it would be years before I saw Jo again. They spent the first night in Santa Monica and headed for Texas the very next day. Tom drove his car. He had to report for active duty in just three days.

Calling on the phone was expensive, so we didn't call often, just at holidays, and Mom spoke most of the time. We just got to say, "Hi, Jo, we miss you. We love you, Jo." One year later, Jo was pregnant—whaaaaat! Jo couldn't get pregnant; she couldn't take care of a child. God had a miracle planned for the two of them. A great miracle.

Jo and Tom engaged

99

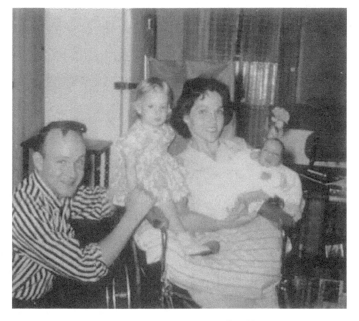

Jo, Tom, Roxanne, and Billy

Jo, Tom, Roxanne, Billy, and Dorothy

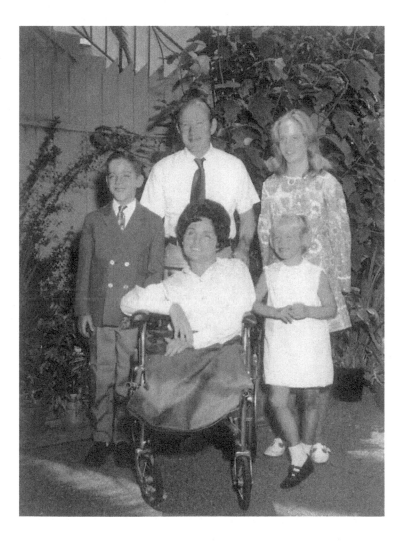

CHAPTER 5

Centinela Southern
Baptist Church

West Los Angeles, California

This little church in WLA played a huge role in the lives of the Jones family. Once Mom started attending this church on a regular basis around 1950, she made sure all of her children attended this church and were active in every phase of its existence.

From as early as I can remember, we attended church on Wednesday night for prayer meeting, Thursday night for choir practice, Friday night for youth night, and Saturday we cleaned the church. Of course, on Sunday, well, we went to church both morning and evening. It became our lives. All of our family and friends attended this church. Mom loved the people here. They all became good friends, shared one another's lives, children, sadness, and joys. The congregation was made up of about one hundred people, give or take, a Sunday. It was small compared to today's megachurches, but everyone knew one another. They were all family, and like any family, there were some rough spots.

The pastors (there were several from 1950 to 1961) gave their all. They definitely preached the salvation story. Sunday morning and Sunday evening, they gave their sermons. I think I heard them all. The wives of these pastors would teach Sunday school and Vacation

Bible School for two weeks during summer. These wives cooked a lot of meals, visited the sick, sang in the choir, raised their children out in public for everyone to see. And if anything went wrong in that family, that seemed to be the gossip for the church members for the next several weeks. It was a tough life. Mom would cook Sunday lunch for not only her family but always invited guests to come and eat with us, sometimes one; but many times, eight to ten people would come and have lunch with us.

Mom would begin cooking every Sunday morning about 5:00 a.m., preparing fresh biscuit. Then she would fry up chicken in a heavy skillet with lard or bacon fat, put the chicken in a pressure cooker, add potatoes, carrots, onion, a lot of salt and pepper; and then she would get dressed and go to church while the pressure cooker slowly cooked all that food. She always made a large green salad, mayonnaise for dressing, homemade jelly for the biscuits, and a lot of iced tea. The family was so happy to get home from church just to smell all that food cooking and steaming in that cooker. Kids ate last at our house. We had to wait until the adults were served; then we could eat. We sat at a table in the kitchen; the adults sat in the dining room.

After dinner would be homemade pies and ice cream for dessert. This was pretty much the main menu every Sunday, but when Mom had a few extra dollars, she would buy two seven-bone roasts and fry those up. The rest of the menu worked well with beef as well as chicken. In my eighteen years at home, I don't think this menu changed. Mom never cooked spaghetti or ham hocks and red beans, or spinach with bacon fat for Sunday; those meals were for the weekly supper only.

The pastors of this church didn't stay long, maybe two to three years at the most. No matter how hard they tried, there was always someone who was judging them on the way they preached, the way they handled or spent the offering, the subject they chose in the Bible. Which chapter and verse was always a big issue. If they became too personal or too judgmental from the pulpit, someone had their toes stepped on, and here we go again, gossip, gossip, gossip. And there was plenty of gossip to go around. All of our family, moms and kids, were saved and had made a personal testimony for Christ in the church. We were all baptized and served in some capacity until we married and moved away. This was Mom's goal in life, to get us all raised in the church, all baptized, all married; and her plan worked very well, until my brother, Buck, became a teenager. He worked at the Santa Monica Pier, and because he was a boy, he got away with a lot of stuff that the girls couldn't do. He would just say, "I'm working with the guys on the boat this weekend," and Mom would say, "Okay, and get home early." But not with the girls, no excuses. You attended church on Sunday, and that was the bottom line.

Sally Meller Jo   Grandma   Lois Trudy

W.L.A. Baptist Church
on Centinela ave
1955

Mother's Day

Mrs. Ellender Jones

Mother of the Year

CENTINELA AVENUE
SOUTHERN BAPTIST CHURCH
Centinela and Santa Monica Boulevard · Los Angeles

Mom's House Shoes

It was a typical Sunday morning in the Jones house. Mom was yelling for everyone to hit the floor; this was her way of saying, "Get up now." It was 6:00 a.m. on a Sunday; why did we have to get up so early? Church didn't start for three hours. The reason, of course, was that we had nine people to get ready for church and only one bathroom. There were girls and one boy, and yes, Mom had to get ready too.

Mom started her day with her bathrobe and old slippers, the slippers that she had had for years. They were dirty take-out-the-trash type of slippers, but they kept her feet warm; and no one can see them, so they were good enough to cook breakfast and get dressed in.

Mom started cooking biscuits and gravy, a staple for our house. Mom made great biscuits from scratch; they would melt in your mouth. We always had gravy made from old chicken grease, flour, milk, and bacon all crumbled up and draining on a paper napkin. She would toss in the bacon for that extra flavor. With sliced and ice-cold cantaloupe, breakfast was on the table. If you were not dressed, you didn't eat. That was the rule, and everyone knew all the rules of the house.

We always took our bath on Saturday nights. We washed our hair too, and Mom would put it up in rag curls. Yes, we went to bed with wet hair, but it was dry by morning, and when the rags were removed, instant curls. Mom made sure we all had a dress that was pressed and ready for church, so we just needed to comb out the curls, brush our teeth, and find our shoes. In this house, we always had one shoe missing. It was under the bed, under the kitchen table, or someone else was wearing it.

The morning was moving along. Just about an hour before our ride to church would show up, while we kids were eating, Mom was helping my sister Jo get ready and get into her wheelchair. She had already had her breakfast in bed. Mom made sure Jo ate first because it took her a little longer to swallow her food and digest it. Jo was trying to comb her hair. It was Buck's turn in the bathroom. He never took a long time. He was the boy; he just combed the flattop and brushed his teeth, and he was ready in a snap.

Marge started to play the piano. We loved to gather around the piano and harmonize until the car came for us. Marge played, and Jo, Lou, and Nora sang songs from the church hymnal. I loved to watch Marge play. She played by ear, and I thought she was terrific to figure out where to put her fingers on the keys and make it sound like the songs we sang at church. Mom yelled out from the back room, "Is everyone ready to go? Check the stove and make sure I turned off the gas." Nora checked the stove, and then we heard the honking of a car out front. It was Mrs. Hungate. She was a lady who lived on the street behind us, and every Sunday morning, she would be out front to take us to church. We had an old car in the garage, but it didn't work anymore. We couldn't afford to have it fixed, so Mrs. Hungate volunteered to see that we got to church on time. There were no seat belts required in the early '50s. We just stacked everyone in, and we sat too deep in the backseat. This meant that six people sat on the backseat. Jo's wheelchair went into the trunk. Jo was lifted into the car and pushed to the middle. Mom got in and put one of the younger girls on her lap, and we were ready to go. Now, you know that there were not nine people in the car from our family. Marge waited at home for her boyfriend, Jack. He would be coming soon to pick her up, and they would meet us at church.

Our church was called Centinela Southern Baptist Church in West Los Angeles. Mom loved this church. She taught Sunday school, took care of the nursery on the third Sunday of each month, and sang in the choir on other Sundays. We arrived at church and began to unload the car. Many friends were gathering around the car and said hi to Mom and Jo. We kids were glad to get out of the car and just run around the parking lot, seeing our friends arrive in the different cars.

Mom said, "I've got to hurry. The choir will be lining up in five minutes." They always entered from the choir door on the right side of the sanctuary. The music would start, and choir folk would march into the choir loft with music sheets under their arms.

"OH NO! NO!"

We all just stopped dead in our tracks. Mom was yelling, "No! I can't go into the choir. I am wearing my house slippers." Mom was so busy getting everyone ready that she forgot to change her shoes, and here she was with those horrible, dirty house shoes on with her best Sunday dress and pearls, and don't forget the pearl earrings.

We all started to laugh; it was so funny. How could Mom walk into the choir room with those terrible slippers on? We were laughing so hard, and Mom was getting mad. "Stop that," she said. "Stop that noise right now. What am I going to do?" Church would be starting in just five minutes, so there was no time to drive back to the house for her church shoes. So today Mom would not be singing in the choir. She was so embarrassed, and she just slipped into the side door of the sanctuary and sat on the back row. When people she knew walked by, they would say, "Ellender, are you okay? You're not sick, are you?" And we would all start to laugh again. When the preacher got up to speak, he kind of smiled and said, "Now, if you had eight kids and you needed to get everyone here on time, then it's possible that you might forget something, so let's go easy on Ellender this morning. The choir is not the same without her." There was no way that Mom would miss church, never. She just sat through the service and hurried right to the car after church and waited in the car until we all collected Jo and all the kids for our ride home.

After lunch, we kids ran to the backyard to play volleyball; and looking down at the step, I could see Mom's house shoes in the trash can. I guess she wouldn't have to worry about making the same mistake twice.

The Television Has to Go Back

A particular Saturday in 1950

This Saturday was going to be different. I knew it from the moment I opened my eyes. I could see Mom standing in the doorway. She woke us every morning, but it was usually just a yell from the kitchen or dining room. But this morning, with her normal rough voice, she said, "You kids hit the floor. We have a lot to do today, and we need to get an early start." Now, this was ordinary for our Monday-through-Friday schedule because we all had to go to school or work. Mom always woke us bright and early, around 6:00 a.m. But today was Saturday, and we normally were able to get that extra hour of sleep. By the time I washed my face, brushed back my hair, and walked into the dining room, Mom was busy ironing. She was always at the ironing board because this was how she earned her living, ironing other people's clothes. We had laundry hanging all over our house. Mom would start ironing about 6:00 a.m. every day except Sunday. Of course, Sunday was the day for her to rest. No, she really didn't rest. She still had meals to cook, a house to clean, and she worked at getting us all ready for church.

But this was Saturday, and I said to her, "Mom, why can't we sleep a while longer? We don't have to go to school." She said, "The social worker is coming today, and we need to get everything ready for her." I didn't know much about the social worker. I was very young, about seven years old, but I knew enough that we were supposed to be afraid. As the other kids started moving around the house, Mom would call out orders, never leaving the ironing board. "Get your breakfast," she would say. "Get dressed and start picking up the house." Scotty Buck was my brother, and he slept on the sofa, so Mom's orders to him was to fold up the sofa and put away the blankets and pick up those jeans on the floor. My brother moved slowly, no enthusiasm from him. He hated housework, and he didn't care who was coming today. He didn't want to clean house.

Jo called from the front bedroom, "Mom, I am ready to get dressed." Mom put down the iron, turned it off, and headed to the front bedroom where my sister Jo slept. Ima Jo had polio. She was paralyzed from the waist down and needed help to prepare her breakfast, comb her hair, and braid it into two long braids, which hung down her back on to her bottom. Jo had always lain on her stomach on her hospital bed, and she used her arms and elbows to support the top part of her body so that she could reach something that she might need or to eat her breakfast. Sometimes Mom would lift her into her wheelchair; then she would push her up to the table to eat. But not today. Everyone was too busy preparing for the social worker, so today Jo ate her breakfast in bed.

We loved to go see Mr. Jimmy. He was the butler and the chauffeur of the rich woman who lived at the top of the hill on our street. We never saw the rich lady. Well, not in person anyway. She had a huge black wrought iron fence around her house and yard that was at least a full block around. We often could see Mr. Jimmy driving up and down the street in a long black car, and we always stood on the sidewalk and waved to him as he passed by. On Halloween night, we would go up to the main gate, ring the bell, and Mr. Jimmy would come to the fence and say, "I know what you kids want. What are you going to say for it?" We all yelled, "Happy Halloween, Mr. Jimmy," and he would give us each a quarter. This was a great treat. We got candy from all the other houses, but Mr. Jimmy would give us money. Mr. Jimmy was a black man, and the only black man I knew. My mom said he was a very special person to be chosen to take care of the rich lady inside the fence.

My sister Jo lay on her hospital bed right by the front window so that she could see outside, and she would wave to people who would come and go by the front of our house. Everyone on the street knew Jo. They would always stop to wave, and sometimes they would come to the door and yell, "Hi, Jo, you doing okay, honey?" We all loved it when company came. We had a big family, and we knew a lot of people, so we were lucky to have a lot of friends who would come to our house. We had seven girls and one boy. My mom was a widow and was struggling to make two nickels stretch to twenty cents. Marge Lucile, Zelma Lou, Eleanor, Ima Jo, Doris Faye, Lois Maye, and Trudy Angela were the girls, and Scotty Buck was my brother. We all lived together in the house on Kensington Road in Santa Monica for a short time. Marge was already dating. Her friend Jack La Vancil was coming around a lot, and my sister Lou had a boyfriend also.

The three girls slept in a bed, Buck on the sofa. Jo was on her hospital bed, and Mom had a bed near Jo in case she might need something during the night. The welfare lady helped us to get clothes and food, and Mom got some money from her to help us with expenses. My mom never said that the social worker was a bad person. She didn't have to. Every time this lady left the house, we would hear Mom crying in the back room. We younger kids just didn't understand why this lady always made our mother cry, but we would hear the older sisters say, "Don't worry, Mom. We can make some extra money babysitting this month or work a few hours' overtime at our jobs to help you with the money problems."

Now, on the particular Saturday, Mom was really nervous. None of us knew why, but we all worked until the lady showed up. Then Mom said, "You kids go out to the backyard and wait until I call you before coming in." We did as we were told, playing a game of hide-and-seek and red rover to kill the time away until Mom told us the coast was clear to come inside.

About an hour had passed when we saw the social worker get in her car and drive away. We waited by the back door, but Mom didn't come. We waited longer; then someone called to her, "Mom, can we come inside now?" My older sister Lou came to the door and let us in. We could see that Mom was crying once again. Doris, Trudy, Buck, and I all stood very still, waiting for someone to speak. Mom looked at us and said, "The television has to go back to the lady on the hill." We all now had tears in our eyes. How could this social-worker lady do this to us? The television was a gift. Mom didn't buy it with food money. Why? Why was she so mean?

Two weeks before this particular Saturday, Mr. Jimmy and the rich lady were driving by as usual, but they didn't just drive by and wave. They stopped the car in front of our house. Mr. Jimmy came up to the door and knocked. My mom went to the door and said hello. Mr. Jimmy said, "The misses has a gift for the little girl in the window. Would it be okay to bring it in?" My mom smiled so big and said, "Sure, please come in." Mr. Jimmy returned to his car, opened the trunk, and lifted out a large cardboard box tied with string and tape. He brought it to the front door and sat it just inside the door and thanked Mom. My mom picked up the box and carried it over to Jo's bed. She said, "Honey, this is for you." Jo was so happy. She waved and smiled at Mr. Jimmy and the rich lady, who was seating in the backseat, and then the car pulled away from the curb and moved slowly up the hill.

When Jo and Mom opened the box, it was a television, with a round glass screen. It was the first television we had ever seen, and we were all so excited. The boyfriends put an antenna on top or our roof and connected the television, and we were able to see *Beany and Cecil* and *Hometown Jamboree* with Tennessee Ernie Ford. Mom could watch wrestling on Saturday night. What a great gift. We were all so excited, and it really kept Jo company while we were at school or at work. Of course, she couldn't watch it while her home teacher was there. Mom set down a few rules that we all were happy to mind. This was a treat, and we didn't want to be punished and not be able to watch this television.

When the social worker came today, she walked around the house as she always did, inspecting the living conditions to see what Mom had spent the welfare check on. Today she saw the television, and she asked, "Where did you get this?" Mom told her that it was a gift from a neighbor lady, but the social worker said, "If you can afford a television, then we don't need to give you so much money." Mom said, "I have barely enough money to feed and clothe my kids now. Please don't take the children's gift away." But the social worker would not listen. She wrote her notes on her spiral notebook and said, "If the television is not gone by Monday, I will reduce your check by ten dollars a month." This doesn't seem like much by today's standards, but in 1950, it was a lot of money.

On Sunday the next day, we all went to church together as usual. Mrs. Hungate, a neighbor and good friend, drove some of our family to church, and Mom had told her about the television that had to be returned. I remember her getting mad and saying that it just wasn't fair to us kids and especially to Jo. Mom had prepared our afternoon meal in the large Dutch oven that she always used when we went to church. She cooked chicken, carrots, and potatoes and diced up some carrots in it. She had made homemade bread, and maybe today we could have ice cream for dessert with homemade peach cobbler.

When the meal was over and the dishes were done, Mom put on her sweater and walked out the front door. She didn't say a word to anyone; we all knew where she was going. She walked up the hill to the big black wrought iron gate and rang the bell. Mr. Jimmy came to the gate. With tears in her eyes, she said, "Mr. Jimmy, we must give back the television. As you know, I am a widowed woman. I have a lot of children to feed, and if I keep the television, the state will cut off my support check, and I can't do that. Please understand that we appreciated this gift so much." Mr. Jimmy just nodded his head, turned, and walked up to the big house. He didn't say a word; he was just very sad. The next day, one of the boyfriends of my older sister packaged up the television and carried it up the hill and left it outside the gate for Mr. Jimmy.

We never met the rich lady on the hill. She was just always there in the big house or in the long black car. Jo continued to wave to Mr. Jimmy and the lady as they drove by. The social worker continued to check on us once a month. Mom continued to iron for sixteen hours a day, six days a week, and she prayed that God would give us a television when the time was right.

A Surprise for Christmas

About 1952

Christmas was always a fun time in our home, but not because we had a lot of presents. We didn't think about getting a lot of presents. We didn't sit on Santa's lap or go shopping. Mom tried to keep the holiday focused on our religious beliefs: Jesus's birthday. This was the reason for Christmas.

Because we were a welfare recipient, our family name was always given to a charitable organization like the Salvation Army or the Elks club. Some very nice people with boxes of food and a gift for everyone would stop by a few days before Christmas. Always, two or three police officers would bring a few presents for the family. The police knew that Mom was alone with a lot of kids. She felt safe with them knowing this information. There was one Christmas that I remember most. Mom had us all lined up, and she introduced us to these visitors, and they gave us each a wrapped gift. I opened mine, and it was a cloth clown doll, and it looked homemade. I felt very special. It was really nice, and I have kept it now for fifty-five years. It still sits on my bed to this day.

I like to think about the person who may have sat with a needle and thread at night, watching TV and making a cute clown doll for a child who didn't plan on getting much for Christmas. I was always very thankful for that gift of love.

A large box wrapped with Christmas paper was full of food items for our Christmas dinner. Turkey, canned sweet potatoes, canned gravy, candy canes, and a bag of hard Christmas candy were some of the gifts. Mom was very grateful for these food items and thanked these good people many times. Mom made us pajamas every year till I was eighteen. They were always soft flannel cloth, and she would pick out pink, blue, or yellow print. She would start sewing in early summer and sewing at night when we all went to bed. Of course, we all knew that the pajamas were for Christmas, and we could see the flannel material stacked up on the sewing machine, but no one said anything. We just tried to ignore it so Mom could feel that she was going to surprise us again for another year.

We were happy to get new pajamas. We lived near the beach, and it was cold and foggy in the winter months. We had a fireplace in the living room where we burned wood and a floor heater in the hallway. But the heater only seemed to warm up the hallway, so the pajamas were clean and warm, and we were very happy to wear them.

Our family had a friend named Dick Schleidt. Dick was a single guy who went to our church and who lived very close to us. He spent a lot of time at our house, and he really wanted to date one of my sisters. But the older girls were too old, and the younger sisters were too young to date, so Dick just came by to visit and help Mom if she needed him for some odd job. Dick always helped Mom buy a Christmas tree and put a stand on it. He would bring his saw and nails and work out on the front grass until the bottom of the trunk was even and would stand up straight. When he was happy with the position of the tree that now stood in the front window of the living room, he took great pride in standing back and enjoying his talent to make the tree look so great.

Dick would always help put the lights on the tree also. Most of us were too short to reach the top, so Dick was right there to stand on the ladder and get that special angel to sit on the top just perfect. We younger girls made paper decorations. We cut our bells, reindeer, and candy canes out of construction paper, sprinkled them with glitter, and hung them with yarn of different colors on the tree branches. Mom loved tinsel, and we could buy tinsel for twenty-five cents a box. So Mom would buy four or five boxes, and we hung the tinsel. When we got bored, we threw the tinsel up in the air, and wherever it landed was good enough for us, but not for Dick. He would take the clumps of tinsel and hang each strand piece by piece. He would say, "You girls should take your time. Christmas only comes once a year."

Bucky bought my mom a gift and brought it home all wrapped in white paper and a bow stuck to the top. He placed it on the mantel of the fireplace and said, "Don't touch. It's breakable." We were all so curious, especially Mom. He was almost thirteen years old and had earned the money for this gift by working at the Santa Monica Pier, so you can understand why he was very anxious about its safety. This gift looked very strange. It was about twenty-four inches long and about three inches wide. It was wrapped but very bumpy-looking, not smooth. We couldn't imagine what it was.

On Christmas Eve, the carolers came to sing in our front yard. This was great because we knew everyone. They were from our church, and they had kids, teenagers, adults, and grandmas singing on our front lawn. Mom made hot chocolate. We stood on the front porch and listened to the carolers; then Mom invited everyone in for chocolate. We just sat around the front room and talked. We were happy to have such nice friends who cared about us and especially

Mom. Everyone loved Mom at the church. She worked hard there, and this was one way they were able to say thank-you.

Christmas morning, we woke early, started to get dressed, and Mom said, "You girls stay in your room for a while." Well, she never said this before. What was up this time? We could hear a lot of moving around, a lot of whispering. It sounded like they were moving furniture. We were trying to hear with our ears pushed up against the door. "Okay, girls, you can come in now." We ran to the living room and were shocked. There were two brand-new wheel bikes, a croquet set (no pieces missing), and lots of wrapped presents under the tree. The entire family was so happy, all hugging and just enjoying the moment together.

Everyone was opening presents, laughing, and talking with excitement. How could Mom afford so many wonderful gifts? We had never seen this many presents. Everyone got new pajamas, handmade by Mom. We were hugging Mom and thanking her for the warmest pajamas ever. Everyone was now settling down. My brother gave Mom his gift for her. None of us could wait to see what was in that white paper. It was a black glass ceramic panther, and it looked like it was stalking something. It was beautiful, and Mom loved it. She said, "Why, this is just great. It will sit on the mantel right here." She placed it up on the mantel like it was a place of honor. And it stayed right there for many years to come; and when Mom moved, that panther went with her to the next house and sat on that mantel.

I remember one more very unusual gift. It was from our friend Dick, and the present was for Doris. This gift's wrapping was very unusual. It had lights on the top that turned off and on like twinkle lights. No electric cord was attached, so what was making these lights blink off and on? Doris finally opened the package. It was several batteries, actually a lot of batteries, some to make the lights work and some just for extra. We looked at one another and said, "What are the batteries for?" Another gift was lifted from under the tree by Mom. There is one more gift for Doris that went with the batteries. We all stood still while she opened that package. It was a table game, and it needed batteries to make it work; so the guessing game, the mystery about the blinking lights, was finally over.

As a family, we loved to play games, especially on Sunday afternoon after church. We rode our new bikes, and we played croquet, volleyball, kickball, jumped rope, whatever games were handy at the time.

This was a special Christmas to remember, so much fun, so much excitement. Mom put the turkey in the oven. She made her own corn-bread stuffing with lots of onions and sage. She pulled jars of home-canned peaches from the cellar to make peach cobbler for dessert. She made homemade bread and opened the cans of yams and added pineapple and marshmallows on the top.

The sun was shining bright on this Christmas Day, a perfect day to play croquet in the front yard. Dick Schleidt came for dinner. He gave Mom a new Bible with her name printed on the front with gold lettering. Lou's boyfriend, George, came, and Marge and Jack also came for dinner. The entire family was all together for this great day. Mom prayed and gave thanks to God for such blessings.

The Baptism

I attended Vacation Bible School on every summer that I can remember. Now, this hasn't been a long time because this story was about when I was seven years old.

Going to church was nothing new to me. My family spent all their extra time at the church. My mom loved to stay involved at the Wednesday night prayer meeting, Thursday night choir practice, Friday night youth night, and my older siblings were able to go out with their friends. Saturday morning, our family helped to clean the church; and of course, on Sunday morning and evening, we went to church.

Now this would seem strange to most people. Maybe you would ask why? But this was perfectly normal for me and my family. My mom was a widow with a lot of kids. She needed all the help she could get in raising these children and keeping them protected and safe, so she stayed involved with the church so she had more control on where we went and who our friends were. If your family was a member of Centinela Baptist Church, then you were probably a good person with Christian values, which was very important to my mother. All my mother's personal friends went to this church, so this was our life growing up. We had a lot of friends, and we had a lot of fun. I was very surprised that other families at my school, John Muir Elementary School, did not have these same practices.

Now getting back to Vacation Bible School, we arrived early every day because my mom was one of the teachers in the children's area, but she was not my teacher. My teacher was Mrs. Sally Miller, and she was the pastor's wife. We began our class time each day with a song, and then we recited a Bible verse, a Bible verse that we practiced every day because at the end of the two weeks of practice, we would say these verses by memory in front of the whole church on Sunday during regular church service. The pressure was intense. Mrs. Miller really wanted to show us off. She wanted to say, "What smart children I have in my class." But I hated getting up in front of all those people. I was very shy, and I did not want to do this thing. I just knew from the very beginning that I would forget a word or scripture, and everyone was going to laugh at me.

Today's lesson was about Jesus letting the children come to him. Mrs. Miller showed us a picture of Jesus sitting on a rock, and the children were all around him, with one sitting on his lap. I listened to her talk very carefully. I really liked this Jesus who wanted to have little children all around him. At our house, children were to be seen but not heard.

We were always sent away when the grown-ups wanted to talk or tell secrets. We always ate last because the adults needed to go on a date, or to work, or do something very important, and the youngest kids could just wait. Now, this was not true with Jesus. Luke 18 verse 16 was one of the verses we had to memorize, and I can't forget it to this day. Jesus said, "Suffer the little children to come unto me, and forbid them not, for such is the kingdom of God."

At the end of her story, she asked us if any of us wanted to accept Jesus into their hearts. If he will let me be close to him, if this Jesus will not tell me to go play outside, if this Jesus died for me so that I could be with him when I died, this is the man for me, so I said yes. I raised my hand and said yes. Mrs. Miller was so pleased, and she gave us all a big hug. She was proud to tell my mom that I had accepted Jesus to come into my heart. Later that day, my mom said to me, "Lois, when do you want to be baptized?" I just stood there. This was not part of Mrs. Miller's story. She never mentioned being baptized, and I said, "No, I don't want to." Mom said everyone needed to be baptized to have Jesus in their heart, but I said, "No way, this is not part of the story."

I had seen my older sisters baptized. This was okay for them, but not for me. I didn't want any part of it, and if someone just mentioned it, I would start crying and run to hide somewhere. They were not going to make me get into that water. I knew why I was afraid to get into the water, but I would not tell anyone. Like I said before, I would just run and hide with just the mention of it.

The years passed, but the pressure never stopped. It seemed like every Sunday or Wednesday night at prayer meeting, the congregation would say that Lois would be baptized. Someone would say, "Don't you want to do what Jesus did?" Or they would say, "This would make your mom so happy."'

I was about nine when Mom sent the pastor of the church, Lloyd Miller, to talk to me. He drove up in front of the house. I was playing jump rope with the neighbor kids, and he called to me, "Lois, can I talk with you for a minute?" I walked slowly to his car. He opened the door and said, "It's okay. I won't keep you long." I got in, sat down, and just looked at the floor.

The pastor began by reading a scripture about being baptized. I started to cry. He said, "Why do you cry every time someone wants to talk to you about this subject?" Well, I had never talked to the pastor by myself. I had never talked to any man except my sisters' boyfriends, and how could I tell him that my family wants me to drown in that water?

I had convinced myself that with fewer children to feed, Mom would not have as many money problems, not as much clothes to buy or food to prepare. One less person would make it easier to sleep at night. We all hated sleeping with three in a bed, and someone always got kicked in the night. My sisters had been teasing me about being so short, and because I didn't know how to swim, they said I would probably drown in that water when I was being baptized. So there was no way I was going to let them do this to me.

The pastor, Lloyd Miller, waited patiently for my answer. Finally, I said, "Maybe I will drown." He said, "What? Is that the problem all this time? You are afraid of the water?" I shook my head yes, and he began to laugh. He said, "Lois, I will not let anything happen to you. I will hold you very tight the whole time, and you can hold on to my hands for the whole time. I would never let you go." I said, "But I am not very tall, and the water is so deep." He said, "Lois, next Sunday, I will walk you into the baptistery. There will not be any water in it, and I'll show you where the water comes to, and you will see that it's not as deep as you think." I said, "Okay, but don't tell my mom or sisters." He agreed.

The next Sunday after church, I quietly went back to where the stairs were and where you entered the baptistery. The pastor met me there just like he promised. Mom was talking to her friends out by the car. She didn't know where I was. The pastor walked down the stairs and then turned and reached his hand out for me. I took his hand and began to walk down the stairs very slowly. My heart was racing so fast; I was so afraid. The pastor said, "Lois, look here. This is where the water will come to, right under your arms. Your head, neck, and shoulders are out of the water, so there's no way that you can drown." Then I said, "But you have to put me in the water." And he said, "Yes, but you will be holding on to me the entire time," and he showed me how my fingers would have a full grasp on his wrist. I said," Okay, I'll think about it." And we both left the church.

It was about a month later when the pastor's message was on being baptized and what that meant. He said, "Baptism doesn't save you. When you accept Christ into your heart, you are instantly saved forever." Baptism was just about joining the church, just being a member of the congregation. The lightbulb went off. All this time, my mom just wanted me to be a member of this church, just to do what Jesus did when John the Baptist baptized him. For some reason, it all just finally made sense to me. No, I am not going to drown. No, I won't make a mistake, and people will not laugh at me. No, the pastor won't let go of my hands. It didn't matter that I was shorter than everyone. *I can do this.*

When the last song was sung, I stepped out into the aisle, walked forward, and told Pastor Miller that I wanted to be baptized. He had the biggest smile, and he just gave me a hug. My sisters said, "So what took you so long? We didn't think this would ever happen for you." I never told anyone why, not even my mom, not my best friend, and the pastor never told anyone either. At the age of ten, I was baptized by Pastor Lloyd Miller. All my family were in the church, and I heard everyone clap when I came out of the water. What a huge relief it was to me that this was over. I did it! I didn't drown, and now people would stop asking me to do it.

Now they just asked me if I would sing a solo—*no!*

Sunday Afternoon Lunch (Which Mom Called Dinner)

At 5:00 a.m., Mom was making homemade biscuits. Kneading the dough was something that Mom has done for years. Everything she cooked was from scratch. She made two pans of hot baked bread before breakfast; the smell was incredible.

"Don't touch that bread," she said. "It is for lunch. We will be really hungry when we get home from church." She started cooking the seven-bone roast and peeling potatoes and carrots to put in the slow cooker with the meat, spices, and lots of onions. Once the slow cooker had started, all the food that Mom prepared went into the cooker. She put on the lid, covered the biscuits with a towel, and let them sit on the top of the stove to cool, but not dry out, before lunch.

The family was getting ready for church, taking turns in the bathroom, ironing that last piece of clothing that someone had forgotten before now. Mom went to the front bedroom and started getting Jo ready. She bathed her with a wet warm washcloth. Then Mom put on Jo's freshly ironed skirt and blouse and her bootie socks that she always wore over her feet, not only to keep warm but because Jo did not like for anyone to see her feet—too many surgeries on her legs and feet. She kept them covered. Mom lifted Jo off the bed and carefully sat her in her wheelchair. Mom helped Jo use her skirt to cover her legs and feet and pushed her over to the mirror so she could brush her hair, brush her teeth, and put on a little makeup.

Mom headed to the back bedroom to start getting dressed for church, all the time yelling at all the kids, "Get your breakfast. Did you find your shoes? Has anyone seen my hairbrush?" Everyone was busy and watching the clock and our ride. Someone from church always gave us a ride. Well, they were always on time, and Mom would never want us to make them late.

Sunday after church was so important to our family. Dinner around the dining-room table was an event. The eight kids, with their boyfriends (maybe just one, but usually at least three), and Mom always invited someone from church to join us for dinner (which was our lunchtime). Mom would make a decision about whom to invite just from conversations at church. Maybe a missionary was in town; they were always the first choice. Maybe it would be the pastor and his wife, and always one of Mom's good lady friends were a definite choice. We were happy to have whoever could come.

The dining-room table was large. We had four matching chairs, but most of the chairs were just metal folding chairs. The adults got to sit in the dining room, and the younger kids had to sit in the kitchen around a corner booth that had a table with built-in benches. Two folding chairs could be fit at the front of the table if needed.

Mom was making a big green salad with plenty of lettuce and tomatoes—homegrown, of course. There were lots of vegetables from our garden, and Mom loved green onions, so they were a must. The biscuits that had been made early in the morning were set in the middle of the table. Butter, salad dressing, and salt and pepper were in place. The older sisters were busy setting the table with plates and silverware—nonmatching, of course. No one cared. There were also glasses for sweet iced tea made by Mom. The roast, potatoes, carrots, and the cooked onions were ready, and Mom called everyone to the table to eat.

Our guest got first choice of where to sit. The older sisters and their dates sat next, and then Mom. We younger kids would just stand around the outside until the prayer was given. Mom would ask our guest to say prayer, and everyone would hold hands. The moment the prayer ended, it was like an explosion of conversation and laughter. Mom had put food on the kitchen table for the younger kids, so now everyone just grabbed a dish of food. It was serve yourself and pass it on to the next. The conversation never stopped. "Jonesy," someone would say, "this dinner is wonderful. This meat is so tender you can cut it with a fork." Everyone was eating and enjoying the food. The biscuit tasted as good as they smelled. The butter just melted on them, and we ate until we were stuffed. Mom said, "I made a cake yesterday for dessert, so save some room." Everyone smiled and just kept on eating.

When everyone at the table had finished, the girls got up and started clearing the table of all the dirty dishes. One sister brought in saucers, and Mom brought in a homemade chocolate cake. All from scratch, of course. Dessert was served (more tea, please). Mom had made plenty for everyone to have as much as they wanted.

The joy of sharing Sunday dinner was an every-Sunday event; not only the food but the conversation was so much fun. Someone always got teased in a great way. We talked about school, friends, new boyfriends, cars, Mom's garden. Everything about our week was mentioned, and everyone was glad to hear the news, good or bad.

After the table was cleared, the dominoes were put in the center of the dining-room table. Again, the older sisters began a game of dominoes; the younger kids played Monopoly in the kitchen after all the dishes were washed by hand, dried, and put away. Mom would take her guests to the living room, which was only five feet from the dining table, and they would talk about church for hours, politics sometimes, and about how well Jo was doing in school. Around 4:00 p.m., Mom would say, "Okay, it is time to get ready for church." That is right. We went to church Sunday morning and Sunday evening. At 5:00 p.m., we were sitting in church once again, singing our favorite hymns and hearing the announcement about the week's activities, and the pastor would start another sermon.

The church family was our family. Mom was loyal to the church, our faith, and all that it stood for. She told us many times that if it were not for the support of the people, friends, from Centinela Baptist Church, she couldn't make it through another week. She was so loyal that we spent Wednesday night at prayer meeting, Thursday night at choir practice, Friday night at youth night (playing games mostly). Saturday, our family cleaned the church for Sunday service; and last, we went to two services every Sunday. This was my life and the life of my siblings until they married.

I remember those lunch (dinner) times with great memories, love for family, for friends. No one cared that our clothes were not perfect. No one cared that our chairs didn't match. No one cared that Mom made fried chicken or seven-bone roast every week because that was what she made the best. We were all there because Mom wanted us all to enjoy what we had, to be thankful for what God blessed us with, to laugh and cry together, to enjoy every moment with Ima Jo (because always in the back of Mom's mind was what the doctors told her: "Enjoy her, she will probably die before she is twenty-one").

Of course, Jo had now passed the age of twenty-one. She went to college. She had a lot of friends, and our family was with her, encouraging her every day. And the boyfriends—oh my gosh, the boyfriends—were always here and taking Jo out to movies, out for a hamburger, just a walk, pushing her down the hill as fast as they could to make her scream with excitement. Our family was so lucky to have one another, to have a mother who knew that family togetherness was the most important thing in life; and no matter where life takes you, you will always have your family to help you, pray for you, support you. Mom gave us the greatest gift of all, and that was one another.

The Criterion Theater

Sunday afternoon, Jo asked Mom if we could go to a movie at the Criterion Theater in downtown Santa Monica. Mom said, "How many of you want to go?" There were Doris, Trudy, Lois, and of course, Jo. Doris was big enough now and strong enough to push Jo's wheelchair two and one-half miles to get to downtown. Mom said okay and gave us enough money to get into the movies, but not enough money for candy, popcorn, or a Coke. And Jo really loved orange Crush pop. We started to look for old Coke bottles that we could trade in at the liquor store, but we couldn't find any around the house, so Doris said, "Let's go, and maybe we'll find some along the street. We'll collect them and turn them in somewhere closer to the movie theater."

We began our walk, and we had just turned the corner when Doris said, "If we hurry really fast, we can ask people for money outside the theater." Now, the idea was that people would see Jo outside the theater in her wheelchair. They would feel sorry for her, and they might give us some money. Mom would have killed us for sure if she had known our plan. Mom had taught us not to beg for anything. This was a really bad idea, but we went along with it because we really wanted some candy.

Doris was pushing Jo really fast, and Trudy and I were almost running alongside her wheelchair just to keep up. This was a very long walk for us but was the only way that we could go to the movies. We did not own a car, and no one was around to drive us.

We finally arrived, and I was so glad to sit down on the concrete pavement in front of the theater. We practically ran the entire way. Now we had to look really sad so someone would give us money. No one smiled. Jo just sat quietly, looking down at her lap; then slowly she would lift her eyelashes in the most desperate way. It wasn't long before people began to stop and give us money. One woman said, "You poor darlings. Who made you sit out here in this hot sun?" My sister Doris said, "We want to take our sister to the movie, but we don't have enough money." The lady said, "Well, how much do you need?" Doris said, "Three dollars." The lady said, "Okay, here is your money. Now take this dear child inside, and you girls have a nice afternoon." Inside, we bought all the candy, popcorn, and a big Coke for us all to share. This was so great. The movie was Elvis Presley's *Love Me Tender*. It was the best movie I had ever seen. Jo thought it was silly; she laughed all the way through it.

On the way home, we talked about what we would tell Mom about our afternoon. There was no way we could tell her about the nice lady who was so generous. No way we could tell her that we had lied. The four of us had to keep this secret forever. We made a pact: no one would tell. And you know what? No one ever told until we were all grown with children of our own, and we laugh about it until this day.

When we finally told Mom, she said, "It's a good thing that I didn't know because I would have beat you and tell God that you had died." I don't know where she got that expression, but she used to say it when she meant business, which was most of the time. I remember when Bill Cosby said to his TV son, "I brought you into this world, and I can take you out." I think it had the same meaning as my Mom's expression, but a lot more tactful.

I don't ever remember begging again. It was just too scary to do over and over, and we knew Mom would find out. Jo went to the movies a lot. She had a lot of boyfriends, not *boyfriend*, but boys who were her friends, and they loved to come to the house to see her. They would take her for a walk to the beach or take her to the movie. Everyone loved Jo. She had the most wonderful smile; it could melt your heart. I always thought she was the most beautiful person I knew. I loved all my family. We always had someone to play with, someone to sing with, someone to watch TV with. But Jo, she was so special. We all just loved being with her and telling our friends that she belonged to us.

A Hole in My Tongue

Most days in our home were just the same: mom at the ironing board, Ima Jo studying in her bed for the next test, the rest of the brother and sisters off to school; and of course, I couldn't find my shoes. Mom yelled at me to hurry up, or I would be late for school. "Where did I put those shoes?" I yelled. "I can't find them." Trudy said, "I think they are under the bed." Sure enough, there they were, hidden with the clothes under the bed. I should have put them away last night, but never mind now. Hurry up!

This was my second year of school, and the best part of my day was playing on the school ground before school started. All my friends would gather to play hopscotch or dodgeball, and we could play for twenty minutes before the first bell rang. I found Michele and Estelle, and we decided to play hopscotch. I had two bobby pins in my pocket to pull my hair back, and I could use those for my lager. Just clip them together, and we were good to go.

We began with Michele. She took the first turn, and now it was my turn. I threw the lager into box one, hopped over one on just one foot, got down to box ten, and started my turn to come back. The next thing I knew, my face was hitting the asphalt ground. It happened so fast my body slammed to the ground. I felt my lip split, and my nose was really hurting. Blood was going everywhere, down my chin, all over my blouse. I know I was in shock, but I didn't know what shock was. Blood was pouring out of my mouth like water. Michele saw this happen, and she ran to get the teacher. My teacher's name was Mrs. Mathes, and she came with some wet paper towels. By the time she found me, I was crying, and all the kids were looking at me, and I could hear them saying, "Oooh, look at all that blood."

Mrs. Mathes helped me up and walked me to the classroom. She said to Michele, "Go find the nurse and tell her to come right away." I was still crying. My lip was swollen, my nose hurt, and the blood in my mouth was finally slowing down. Mrs. Mathes laid me on one of the rest mats on the floor. She kept putting cold wet paper towels on my mouth. The swelling was getting bad; it felt like a large hard grape on my tongue. My tongue was so thick and hurt I was having a hard time talking.

The nurse soon arrived, helped me up, and together we walked to the school office. Everyone was staring at me. I just kept crying. The nurse laid me on a bench in the office and said, "Don't move. I am calling your mother."

Betty Foley lived next door to us, and she had a car. Mom called her, and they both came to get me. Mom took one look at my face, and she said, "Good Lord, what has happened to you?" I heard the nurse talking to Mom, saying, "She needs to see a doctor right away. I think there is damage to her tongue." Mom said, "What happened?"

The nurse said, "She tripped on her shoelace playing hopscotch." I don't remember tripping, but my shoelace was untied.

We arrived at the doctor's office, which, years later, I learned was the emergency room. What does a second grader know? To me, it was a man with a white coat whom I didn't know. He was looking at my face, and he said for me to open my mouth. "Mrs. Jones," he said, "this young lady has bitten a hole clear through her tongue. If I stitch it, there will be a knot on her tongue forever. I think we should just put ice on it and let the swelling go down and hope that it will heal itself."

My face was a mess. My lip, tongue, and the side of my nose were all damaged and swollen. The doctor put a thick pack of ice on my lip and said I could eat only ice cream for the next couple of days.

Betty drove us home. Jo was with her home teacher, Mrs. Deichman, and when they saw me, I could see the horror on their faces. Jo said, "Come here, sugar." I went and stood by her bedside. She had me lie my face down in front of her on the bed, and she stroked my head and kissed my forehead. Anytime I was with Jo, I felt good. Mom said, "Lois, just crawl upon that bed over there and go to sleep for a while. I'll get you more ice."

I didn't go to school for the next few days; I just stayed home with Mom and Jo. It took some time for the swelling to go down. My tongue hurt for a long time, but I still had to go to church on Sunday. No matter what happened, we always went to church on Sunday.

Measles

Fourth grade, John Muir Grammar School
Santa Monica, California

There were so many people absent from class from the measles outbreak that was going through the school, and everyone was talking about it. But so far, I still hadn't got them, and I thought that this was just great. My neighbor Carol had them. I had gone over to see her, and Mom said, "Well, now you're going to get them for sure." Measles is infectious and easily given from one person to the next.

Several weeks had passed, and the teacher had stopped talking about the measles outbreak. Most of the kids in my class had their time at home and now returned to school. It just seemed like a normal school day now. Mom kept saying, "Lois Maye didn't get the measles. Maybe this outbreak is going to pass her this year." I had a big smile on my face, sounded great to me.

Now the school year was just about over. The month was May, and we were getting ready for summer vacation, report cards would come out soon, and we needed to finish up all the final tests for the year. Class pictures were done, and the teacher had gotten the printouts of the class picture along with the report card.

Just one more week and summer vacation would begin. I was excited about Vacation Bible School week at church, and maybe this year, I would be able to go to summer camp. In the morning before school started, only three days before school ended, I noticed I had a red rash on my right arm. It was itching; of course, I scratched it. It just got redder. I thought that it was probably from playing four square with my friends before school. By the time I got home from school that day, my neck was itching and around the back of my right ear. I didn't say anything to Mom and just went about my normal routine of picking up my room and helping Mom start dinner.

By the time evening came, I really didn't feel well. I just wanted to curl up on the sofa with a small blanket on me, watch a little TV with Mom, and go to bed early; but when I got off the sofa, my arms and legs were covered with red rash. I said to Mom, "I am itching all over me, and I don't feel good." She took one look at me and said, "Oh Lordy, you've got the measles." I said, "Are you sure?" She said, "Go look it in mirror, and it looks like a bad case. Well, it took you long enough to get them. And now you can't go to school anymore. It takes a good week to get over the rash and wait for your skin to scab over. Get your pajamas on and get in the bed in the back bedroom. You can't sleep in the kids' room until this is over." I hated the back bedroom. I was scared in there. This was the room where the man tried to climb into our window.

Mom gave me some medicine by mouth to help with the itching, and I could hear her telling everyone at dinner that I had the measles and I couldn't come out of the back bedroom for a week. I just lay there and cried—no school-end party for me. Who would get my report card and my picture? I won't be able to say good-bye to my friends or my teacher.

The next morning, I looked in the mirror, and I was covered in red dots all over me. My eyes were swollen. I had rashes between my fingers and toes, under my arms, and my back and chest were just covered. I looked terrible. My mother brought me something to eat for breakfast, toast and peanut butter, but I didn't want to eat.

Everyone told me, "Don't scratch. It will leave scars if you do." I was so itchy it was really hard not to scratch. The doctor made me sleepy, so I slept for most of the first two days. By the third day, school was over, and my friend Carol came to see me. It was okay for her to come in because she had already had the measles herself, and you couldn't get them twice. We played games together, dominoes and tic-tac-toe. She brought my report card and my class picture, and I was the only person who got the measles at the end of the year. Mom never knew why it took me so long after everyone else had gotten them. By the end of the next week, it was over. I was covered in scabs and was able to eat with the rest of the family, come out of the scary bedroom, and take a bath. Now my summer vacation could begin.

Breast Cancer

Santa Monica, 1956

I was thirteen years old and in the seventh grade at John Adams Junior High School. Santa Monica, where we lived, was about half a mile or more, approximately seven long blocks, away. I would leave my house, cross Lincoln Boulevard at the light, and head up the hill to Sixteenth and Pearl. I only had a few friends in this year of my life. I was terribly shy and afraid of everyone. My girlfriends from grammar school had already spread out to meet new girls or boys, and many had friends from their neighborhood who went to John Adams also, so they would hang out with them.

Many of the girls I knew from John Muir Grammar School were developing a lot faster than I was. I would overhear conversations about their new bras and how their bodies were really looking different. They said that now they wouldn't be embarrassed when changing clothes in the locker room for PE (physical education) class. In the first six years, the teachers never asked us to change clothes at school, just once. There was a time when one of the teachers had found a Girl Scout uniform that she thought would fit me, and she asked me to put it on in the bathroom. That was embarrassing. But now everyone was showing off their new bras in gym class, not me. I usually hid behind the curtain in my dressing stall. I didn't want anyone to see what I was wearing. I really didn't need a bra. I was still flat as a pancake, but Mom felt that if you're in seventh grade, you should show a little modesty.

The bad thing was that we couldn't afford a new bra for me, so Mom took some bras that my sisters had worn and grew out of, and sewed them up for me. She tried to make them fit, but they looked awful. I wore them, but no one was ever going to see them. She took the cup of the bra and sewed it straight across the center and cut off the excess. Then she took the side panels and sewed up two inches, one inch on both sides. They were not only terrible-looking; they were uncomfortable, and the straps wouldn't stay on my shoulder no matter how I tried to adjust them. I was a nervous wreck on most days during my three years in junior high. I just didn't want anyone to notice me or laugh at me.

Christmas came and went, then January and February. Spring was definitely blooming in all the front yards on Pearl Street. I loved to look at all the pretty flowers along that street. You would think everything was just fine, but it was not fine at my house. The older sisters were whispering a lot. Conversations would stop when I walked into a room. They would stare at me until I walked out of the room, and then the conversation would begin again. Very softly, I tried to hear; and once in a while, I would get a few sentences like, "She's only going for a test. The doctors aren't sure. Pastor Miller will drive her to the hospital." Two mornings later, Pastor Miller came to our door very early. It was before we left for school. Mom gave us all a kiss. She told Marge to make sure we—as in Buck, Doris, Trudy, and myself—got to school on time. I asked Doris, "Where's Mom going?" She just shrugged her shoulders and said, "I don't know."

As I was leaving for school, I heard Jo and Lou talking about Mrs. Phipps or Mrs. Miller bringing our dinner over later in the afternoon. That night at dinnertime, once again, I asked, "Where's Mom?" Marge said, "She is in the hospital. She is having surgery. Now eat your dinner and go get a bath." I couldn't eat, and when I got into the bathtub, I just sat and cried. Everyone I knew who had gone to the hospital had died. Was Mom going to die?

Marge took care of Jo on most days. Marge, Lou, and Nora all had after-school jobs, so everyone was gone from the house most of the day. Mrs. Deichman was Jo's home teacher, and she came about 10:00 a.m., and she stayed till about 2:00 p.m., giving Jo her high school classwork for each day. Jo loved her teacher. She was learning so much, and Jo just loved to study and to read.

The social worker stopped by to see us on two different occasions. Of course, she didn't talk to us kids. She sat with Lou, Marge, and Jo and was updated on Mom's progress. Of course, it was all hush-hush; very quiet voices came from that room.

Two weeks had passed, and Mom still wasn't home. The ladies from the church were still bringing in our evening meal, and we were always glad to have company. It was so strange without Mom, no one cooking in the kitchen, no laundry hanging all over the house. Maybe Mom had died, and no one would tell me. No one answered my questions. They would ignore me and just change the subject. I wanted to have Mom at home. My shoe had a hole in the bottom of the sole on my left foot. I would cut out a cardboard piece and slide it into my shoe so that I could wear them the next day. Marge would play the piano at night. She would play from the church hymnal, and all of us kids would gather around the old upright piano that had been given to us, and we would harmonize with the songs we loved and knew so well. Jo sang soprano, Lou sang alto, and the rest of us just did the best we could.

I was not a good student. I felt confused a lot of the time at school, not really understanding where I was supposed to be or the assignment that needed to be turned in. I did okay in PE, home-making, and typing, but science and math were very difficult. And everyone at home was so busy with their own homework, cleaning the house, taking care of Jo that I just didn't ask for help. I just felt it wasn't fair for them to help me.

On this particular Friday, we had a test in science. I studied the chapter, read it over and over, hoping that I could get a passing mark. On Monday, the teachers handed out our test score. When he handed me my test, he smiled at me. His name was Mr. Jones. I liked him a lot. I looked at the paper, and there was an A. I couldn't believe it. I never got an A before. I rushed home after school to tell someone about my grade. I wanted someone to be happy for me.

As I walked into my yard, I saw a lot of people standing around the front of the house; there were a lot of cars on the street and in our driveway. I walked upon the porch. My heart was pounding. Something had happened to Mom. Was Mom dead? Who was going to tell me the bad news? I walked into the foyer of the house and looked into Jo's bedroom. Jo smiled and said, "Honey, Mom's home."

I looked around and saw about twenty people standing around the room, and as they moved away, I could see Lou's bed on the other side of the room, and Mom was lying in the bed. I dropped my books and ran to the bed, falling on my knees and putting my arms around her. I was crying, Mom was crying, I think everyone was crying by now. Mom said, "Be careful, honey, not to touch my left side." She was all bandaged up. There was gauze across her chest, under her left arm, and the thigh of her left leg was bandaged also, thick white gauze with a lot of white tape. I said to Mom, "What did they do to you?" She answered, "I'll tell you later."

I got up and picked up my books and papers. I showed Mom my A on the science test. She said, "That's fine, that's really fine." Then I said, "I've got a hole in the bottom of my shoe, and it has got-ten so big that cardboard won't work anymore." Everyone started to laugh, and Mom said, "We'll see about getting you some new shoes." Then they began to change the bandages. I was close by and could see her flesh. They really cut her to pieces. They took the breast off down to the chest bones. They cut out the lymph glands and muscle from under her left arm, leaving her this huge hole under the armpit and down about three inches into her left underarm. They sliced off some skin from her upper thigh and used it to cover the wounds, and she had hundreds of stitches. I was in shock. How could they do this to my mom? I didn't know what cancer was. I didn't know what breast cancer was and how dangerous it was. She was in a lot of pain and ate most of her meals in bed. For a long time, many neighbors and friends came to visit, bringing food, flowers, and candy for the kids.

We were all happy when Mom could sit up and eat at the table with the rest of the family, and happier when she was able to cook red beans, corn bread, and fried chicken. No one cooked like our Mom. When we found Mom in the kitchen or standing at the ironing board, then we all knew that life was getting back to normal for us, as normal as this Jones family could get.

A few months went by, and Mom was fitted for a false breast. It was a heavy silicone gel in a bag, and it fit into a pocket that was sewn inside her bra. She was later known as high pockets because she kept her money and her keys inside the pocket also. Mom lived to the age of eighty-nine, and every five years, a nurse from the general hospital would call us just to see how Mom was doing. We were very happy to say that she was still living.

I don't blame the doctors at the general hospital, but I don't believe that she ever had cancer. The doctors were just learning about breast cancer. They were so afraid of this diagnosis; it was a death sentence for most women. Mom had fallen on the steps of the Los Angeles courthouse. She bruised her breast badly, and that was when they noticed a lump. The doctors were doing experimental surgery, and I am sure they did the best that they knew how. But when the nurse called us to find out how Mom was doing, she told me that most the women with breast cancer had died in five years. They were always amazed that Mom was doing so well.

The hospital did not have mammograms. They did not have MRIs or scanning equipment. It was just a guessing game. The doctors at the general hospital were not specialists; most were just interns learning their skills. And all welfare patients who could not afford medical insurance had to go to this hospital for treatment. Mom always said the nurses were wonderful to her.

My Brother, Bucky, and the Lobsters

My brother, Buck, was older than me by three years. He really didn't spend much time at home once he became a teenager. He just wanted to work at the Santa Monica Pier. After school each day, he would go down to the pier to work. He would find odd jobs and sometimes worked on the fishing boats.

I do remember that many times, he smelled bad, and Mom would say, "Buck, get in that bathtub. You're not sleeping on the sofa smelling like that." Somewhere along the time of working at the pier, Buck met a man named Fran Winberg. This man became good friends with my brother; and later, after graduation and returning from his duty in the coast guard, Buck and Fran became partners in the boating business. Buck studied very hard to pass the ship captains' test. He just wanted to be the captain in the worst way, and he did pass, and Mom was so proud of him.

Now, getting back to the fish story, I need to back up a little and tell you that our house was great, but we had problems with cockroaches. Sometimes, when we got up at night to use the bathroom, we would turn on the light, and the roaches would scatter on the floor. Mom did what she could to get rid of them, but living close to the beach, this was a constant problem for our family. I was terrified of these horrible bugs and many times would stand in the hallway for a long time, almost peeing my pants before turning on the light, knowing that I would probably see one of these disgusting bugs. And this is why this story is so important.

One day, I returned from school. I believe I was in the ninth grade, and I tried to open the front door, but it was locked. So I walked down the driveway to the back door, and the door was standing open. I entered through the service porch and started to put down my books on the table when I saw two large red roaches, each about twelve inches long, crawling across the floor. I screamed a most horrible scream and ran terrified from the house. I could hear my mother calling my name, "Lois Maye, come back! Where are you going?" I ran to our neighbor's house, crying, shaking, and barely able to get a word out. Betty Foley let me into her house, and she held me in her arms. She kept saying, "Good Lord, what has happened?"

Soon my mother came for me. She said, "Those are not cockroaches. Those are lobsters from the Santa Monica Pier. Buck brought them home for dinner." She couldn't have said anything worse; there was no way that I could eat something so horrible. She told me that Buck was fishing with a man at the pier, and this man gave Buck two lobsters for the family dinner. Well, I had never heard of such a thing. We never ate fish; Mom didn't cook fish. Chicken and seven-bone roast were the main dinner for our family. Sometimes hot dogs and maybe hamburgers, but certainly not these things that looked like cockroaches and crawling on our floor. And there was no way that I was going back into that house until those things were gone.

I stayed with the Foleys for two nights, and Betty drove me to school with her girls so I could get over the fear. I finally went home by the weekend, and my brother laughed at me. In fact, all my siblings laughed about this, but I never forgot. To this day, I will not eat lobster or sit with anyone who eats lobster. I've been known to get up and leave a restaurant if I see a lobster tank.

I don't remember my brother ever bringing home lobsters again, and I was a senior in high school when I finally agreed to go down to the pier for the first time, and I saw the fish market with all the live and fresh fish that was displayed on iced shelves.

Our family had a good friend from church. His name was Walter Vermillion, and Walter loved to deep-sea fish. One summer, his niece was visiting from Tennessee. She was my age, and Walter asked my mom if I could go fishing with them on a fishing boat leaving from the Santa Monica Pier. I agreed. I thought maybe this would help my fear, so off we went, the three of us. Walter showed us how to use the fishing poles and how to load the bait onto the hook. I was feeling a little sick by watching this hook thing, but I held the pole; and when the boat stopped, we were told to lower our lines.

By now, I was really sick and needed to throw up, so Walter held my line as I ran to the bathroom. When I got back to my place along the rail, the captain told me to stay outside because going below would just make me a lot sicker. I held the pole and kept throwing up over the rail. When the captain said we were moving and to pull in our lines, my hooks were loaded with fish. I was so sick I didn't even feel the pulling on the line. I was the only one of the three of us to catch anything on this day. I never went fishing again. I didn't think this was a lot of fun, but I did learn what turning green meant.

Pretty Boy (Parakeet)

Mrs. Deichman, Jo's home teacher, came twice a week to give Jo her school lessons. Jo studied all the time and was always ready for more; she loved to learn. When Mrs. Deichman came into our house, we all scattered so the house was quiet for the two of them. Mrs. Deichman set up her books on a small table close to Jo's bed, and we could hear her explaining math, history, English, whatever the lesson was for that day. Jo never complained about anything, and she never had a bad word about schoolwork.

Jo had received a special gift from our brother-in-law Jack La Vancil. It was a parakeet to sit by her bed and keep her company. Jack clipped the wings of this bird and sat him on a perch by Jo's bed. Jo would talk to this bird all day: "Hello, Pretty Boy," "Good morning, Pretty Boy," "Where are my kisses, Pretty Boy?" The bird would jump up on Jo's bed and walk around chirping. He would sit on her shoulder or her finger, and they would just talk to each other. Sometimes he would pull on the strings from the blanket or sheets. Everyone knew that Jo loved this bird, and we all enjoyed watching her talk to him, play with him, and even sleep with him.

Mrs. Deichman was not as fond of the bird as Jo. Pretty Boy would jump on her paperwork or books and leave her a little present. She would say, "This dang bird has done it again. Look at this mess." Jo would laugh, and Mom would put the bird back on its perch and hand Mrs. Deichman a Kleenex.

Jo taught Pretty Boy to talk, and talk he did, all day long. He would say, "Good morning," "Wake up, Jo," and the best part was when he would say, "Hide the whiskey, boys. Here comes the preacher." I don't remember him saying the complete sentence, but he could say, "Hide the whiskey." He could get *preacher* out very clearly.

This was Jo's special friend, and the rest of us needed to ask permission before we could handle Jo's bird. We wanted to put the bird on our shoulder and walk around the house with him. Jo would say, "Bring my bird back where he belongs *now*." Sunday morning, we all got ready for church just like we did every week. We heard the horn honking out front of the house, and we knew it was time to go. We had a lovely morning at church, and everything seemed so normal.

When we arrived in front of the house, we noticed immediately that the front door was open. No one remembered who shut it or who the last one was out of the house. We all said the same thing, "Hope Pretty Boy is okay." We ran to the house while Mom lifted Jo into her wheelchair. We started looking for Pretty Boy, but we couldn't find him. Not on Jo's bed, not on the floor, and not on his perch. Jo started to cry. "Oh no, my bird is gone. My beautiful bird is gone." We all cried. How could this happen? Everyone had been so careful with the door ever since we got this bird.

Mom was sure she locked the door, so who came into our house while we were gone to church? We never locked our back door because there was always someone in the house, and we never felt threatened. Someone left the door open; we never found out who that was.

Jo didn't want another bird. Jack tried to give her another, but she just said, "No thanks, my friend is gone. I just want to remember him." Mom said, "Jo has gone through a lot of tough times, but this one hurt her so much." It just wasn't fair.

Mother of the Year Award

May comes around every year, and Mother's Day comes with this month every year. Our church, Centinela Baptist Church of West Los Angeles, wanted to do something very special for the moms of the church, so they started an event called Mother of the Year Award. It was a huge honor to receive this award; it was not given lightly. The church deacons would gather and would accept suggestions from the congregation on which women would receive this honor in May on Mother's Day Sunday. I remember Sally Miller receiving this award. She was the pastor's wife, and she was active in every part of the church and was probably more active than her husband, the pastor. She led Vacation Bible School each year and would drive a bus around town collecting all the children, with the parents' permission, to come every day for two weeks and enjoy the stories from the Bible, contests, and sports activities. She was really an amazing asset to this church.

Another person who won this award was Mable Broussard. She also was very active, and she was the secretary of the church and personal secretary to Pastor Lloyd Miller. She typed the bulletin each week and made sure the offering was posted for all to see, and she contacted other churches in the area for joint activities. But this year was May 1954, and we had no idea who would receive the award. It was amazingly quiet; no one was saying a word. We, the Jones kids, really loved Mother's Day. We made it as special for Mom as possible. She didn't have to cook on this day, she was always given a corsage from a florist, and none of us missed church on this day. It was my mom's hope and dream that all her children be Christians, to love the Lord and be baptized. This was her day.

We arrived at the church just like we always did, and Mom headed for the nursery. It was her turn to take care of the nursery during Sunday school today, and we kids headed for our individual Sunday school classes, and still no one had said a word about who would receive the award. Yes, we asked, but people would just shrug their shoulders or say, "I don't know." We headed for the church service and entered through the front door of the church. Lots of people were there. The seats were filling up fast, and Sally said to me, "Lois, why don't you sit down front today? I think your mom will be sitting toward the front also." "No," I said, "she will probably go to the choir." "No, dear," she said, "not today. Today is special." I took the bulletin from the usher and looked at it.

"Mrs. Ellender Jones, Mother of the Year," and there was a picture of my mom on the front of the bulletin. I got tears in my eyes, but I didn't want anyone to see me crying. I was eleven years old and very shy, so I quickly started walking to the front of the pews. I didn't see Mom anywhere, but my sisters and my brother were down front, and I went to sit with them. Of course, they were as surprised as I was. And now where was Mom?

Pastor Lloyd Miller got up to speak and said, "Ellender is still in the nursery. We've sent a person to release her from her job there. We set this up on purpose so she would be surprised." Just at that moment, Mom walked through the side door, and everyone stood and started to clap for her. Her friend Sally handed her the bulletin, and for the first time, Mom saw her picture and read the words "Mother of the Year." She began to cry. Pastor Lloyd walked down to her and put his arms around her shoulders and said, "This is a great day, Ellender. We are so proud of you."

Inside the bulletin, it read, "1954, Mother of the Year. Our mother of the year is Mrs. Ellender Jones. She is the mother of eight children. Both Mrs. Jones and all the children are most active in every phase of our church life. We honor this courageous mother who, to all of us, has been an inspiration and a blessing. Her home is a Christian home. Her life is a testimony of what the Lord can do with a willing, determined Christian. It's not what you possess but what you do with what you have which determines your true worth on earth."

The music began to play. Everyone stood and sang "Faith of our Mothers."

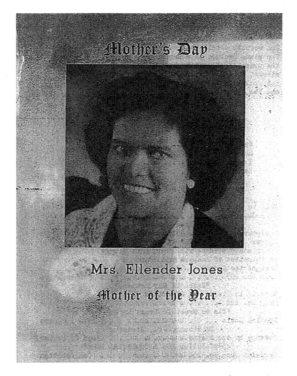

Mrs. Ellender Jones
Mother of the Year

The pastor's message was, "A prescription for a Christian home." Mom was awarded a new Bible (King James, of course) and another corsage from the church, so she looked great with two corsages on her jacket and a new Bible in her hand. She was so proud, so honored, and she was happy that she was loved by so many people. After that great day, Mom became more involved in the church (if that were possible). She said, "I want to make sure I am worthy of this great honor they gave me." After about the third year, we said, "Okay, enough, you don't have to prove anything anymore." We would all laugh, and she would just say, "Oh flitter." This was her famous expression when she couldn't think of anything else to say.

A Gift for Ruth Cook Beaman

This story is the most recent in my collection of memories because I received a Christmas card from Ruth Cook Beaman. Ruth is a person I knew for only a short time, yet she has left an event in my life that has touched my heart so deeply and has moved me to tears on many occasions.

Ruth was a girl I knew from elementary school, John Muir Grammar School in Santa Monica, California. Ruth was in my same class for second, third, fourth, fifth, and sixth grade. I rarely saw her in junior high school, John Adams Junior High. She had found a new set of friends, and I knew her only as an acquaintance through high school, which was Santa Monica High.

Getting back to this event I spoke about earlier, when I was ten years old, Ruth gave me an invitation to her birthday party. Now, as I told you before, I was very shy and never went to any of my friends' homes. This was the first invitation I had ever received at school, and I was very nervous about it and at the same time excited. I ran home after school that day and asked Mom if I could go to her party. My mom said, "Lois, I don't have money for any birthday present. Sorry, you need to stay home and help me with the babysitting job I have on Saturday."

I was disappointed but also relieved. Now I didn't have to be embarrassed about being shy and really afraid to walk to a different house that I had never been in before. I didn't speak about the invitation again during that week, but on Friday evening, Mom had some money given to her for ironing the neighbors' clothes, and she walked to the market to buy groceries. When she returned home, she said, "Lois, I have a surprise for you. You don't have to babysit tomorrow, so you can go to your friend's birthday party."

"No!" I said. "I can't. I don't have a present." Mom said, "It is okay. I had two dollars left from the groceries, so I bought your friend a gift." Then she showed it to me. I stood very still. I didn't say a word. *What do I do now?* was my thought. Mom had bought a cup and saucer for her gift. It was white with gold trim around the top edge of the cup and the plate, and it had a garden scene on the side of the cup. On the bottom of the plate, it said, "Made in China." How could I tell my mom that no child wants a cup and saucer for their tenth birthday, especially since she bought it from the local market? It would be great if it was a hair barrette, or a doll, or maybe some jewelry, but I never dreamed it would be a cup and saucer.

Saturday morning, Mom wrapped the cup and saucer in tissue paper and put them in a box. Then she tied a red ribbon around the box, a ribbon that was left over from Christmas wrappings. "There," she said, "all ready to go." I wanted to cry. I didn't want to go. Everyone was going to laugh at me for such a stupid gift. I was laughed at a lot, but not today, not in front of my friends.

I left for the party at twelve noon, walked the four blocks to Ruth's house, and when I saw the house, I just froze on the sidewalk for a long time. I just couldn't go in.

I finally knocked at the door, and Ruth opened the door for me. I said, "I cannot come to your party because I have to babysit." I gave her the gift and ran down the street. I walked to the playground close by and sat on the swing for about one and a half hour, and then I went home. Mom said, "Did you have a good time?" "Yes," I said, "I did have a very good time." I never mentioned to anyone again about that cup and saucer. Never, not in junior high or high school. I just wanted to forget all about it.

In 1986, my husband and I received an invitation to the twenty-fifth class reunion of my graduating class, and we decided to go. My childhood was many years behind me. I had not seen most of my classmates for many years, and it was exciting to go and see how everyone looked after twenty-five years. As they called out the names of the class members, Ruth Cook's name was mentioned. I had heard she had moved to Texas with her husband, Bernard and that he had become a minister, but she did not answer when her name was called. Later in the evening, someone told me Ruth was coming back to Los Angeles area to visit her sister. Maybe, just maybe, we could find her and meet up and have lunch together.

Later the next week, we did meet up with Ruth's sister's house in the San Fernando Valley area. My friend Michele picked me up, and my husband, Dale, watched the children. For the first time in twenty-five years, I would see Ruth Cook, someone whom I liked very much in my grammar school days.

While sitting in the Jacuzzi, drinking wine, Michele, Ruth, and I were chatting about days long past—kids, jobs, husbands, etc. Ruth said, "Lois, do you remember the last time we were really close friends?" I said, "No, I can't remember." She said, "It was at my birthday party. You brought me a gift, but you couldn't stay for the party, do you remember? Lois, you gave me a cup and saucer for a gift, and I still have it. It was the only gift that I remember from that party. I just love it. My mom said how wonderful that your mother was able to buy a gift. We all knew how hard she worked by ironing all those clothes." I was speechless. I didn't know she liked it. All the years that had passed, and because of my own fears, I had missed out on having a good friend because I was embarrassed.

I told Ruth the truth, and the tears flowed. We both felt it was such a shame that we hadn't spoken about that event for so many years. Who knew what might have happened if we had?

Ruth and I have written many times over the last years, mostly Christmas cards; and just two days ago, I received a new Christmas card from her. The letters read that she was well. She couldn't believe that we were going to be sixty-six years old soon; also the entire class of 1961 would be sixty-six years old. She still lives in Texas with her husband, Bernard.

By the way, she still has the cup and saucer I gave her fifty-five years ago. She says she looks at it often and remembers her class friends from John Muir Grammar School. And she never forgot how hard my mom worked so she could have such a lovely gift.

Update on my friend Ruthie in Texas
September 14, 2010

My friend Michele has just retired from the Boeing Aircraft Company. She had worked there for forty-eight years, a huge achievement for her and her husband, Bob. I decided to give Michele a surprise party for this great occasion, so I called Ruth in Texas and asked her to come. She could stay with me at my home in Riverside, California, and we could go to this party together. Ruth said yes. I was thrilled and excited. I picked her up at the Ontario Airport near Riverside, and she spent two days with me, helping with the final details of the party. Michele was shocked when everyone yelled, "Surprise!" in her house. She had gone out shopping, and when she got home, the house was full of family and friends. Many of our classmates came also.

Michele almost fainted when she saw Ruthie standing in her living room. What a great surprise, a great night to remember. We kidnapped Michele from her house that very evening, and she spent the weekend with Ruth and me at my home in Riverside. We had three days together. We know we will be friends forever.

Just this week, years later after Michele's party, Ruth sent me a picture of the cup and saucer. It still sits in her china closet. God is so good to give me a friend for so many years. We are both so grateful for the love we share, even now 2016.

The Foley Family

Bob, Betty, Carolann, and Linda lived next door to us in Santa Monica on Kensington Road. The only thing separating our two families was a gravel driveway. Bob worked as a milkman for a local company. He left early every morning, came home early afternoon, and always took a nap. Betty, a homemaker caring for her two daughters, drove a large Cadillac that she always parked in front of her house on the street, not in her driveway.

Carolann was one year younger than me. She was four years old when we met them for the first time, and Linda was one year younger than Trudy, my youngest sister. Linda was three years old. In the early years that Betty was not in our house at some time during the day, she and Mom became very good friends. Sometimes when I left for school in the morning, Betty came by for breakfast and would talk with Mom. My mom didn't drink coffee, so Betty would bring her cup from home, and sometimes she would just sit with Jo in Jo's bedroom, just passing the day away visiting. She always stopped by at dinnertime to say hello to all of us and many times would sit down and enjoy dinner at our table.

My mom didn't have a car, so Betty drove her to town or to the market during the week. We kids played together every day. Carol and Linda had more things (toys) than we did, but we had a big family, so they were able to always have someone to play with. They also helped us with our chores so that we could go play a lot sooner. Betty was a good friend to Mom and helped her with sewing Easter dresses and cutting out patterns. Mom did all the Foleys' ironing, and Betty would sit with Mom while she ironed those clothes, and they would talk about everything.

Marge (my oldest sister) and Jack were now married, and we enjoyed the luxury of their house on many weekends. Marge wanted a baby very badly, and she did get pregnant. We were so thrilled and excited—Mom's first grandchild. But the baby died at birth from hyaline membrane disease. The baby's lungs were too weak, and he died. He was a seven-pound baby boy, and they named him Jack. We all were so devastated, the first death in our family. Betty was right there for us, bringing us food and taking Mom where she needed to go in her car. Betty's family came to the funeral and took care of us. I remember after the funeral, I was crying, and these large arms wrapped themselves around me and hugged me tight. It was Betty, and I never felt safer.

For the second time, Marge was pregnant, nine months of excitement, baby clothes, baby showers. Once again, the big day came, but the baby only lived a few hours. Betty and her girls got us through a week of heartbreak. We thought we would never stop crying.

In junior high school, around the ninth grade, our relationship with the Foley family began to change. We had a lot of friends at our church. These friends would come to our house on Sundays, and we would all go to the beach together The Foleys did not go to our church. All of our free time became church-directed, and the Foley family went about their lives. We only say them at school. As Trudy, Doris, and I moved into high school, Betty did not come over anymore. There were no more breakfasts together, and we never saw her at dinnertime either. Our lives were all so busy. We had after-school jobs. I was working for Pacific Telephone Company as a long-distance operator, and I had a new boyfriend named John. My sister Doris was dating Calvin, and they were engaged to be married as soon as she graduated. We would double-date with our siblings, but not with the Foley girls.

Jo was off to college at Riverside Baptist University. Lou and Marge were now married; maybe even Nora was married at this time. I was now in the tenth grade. I rarely saw Carolann at school. We had different friends, different classes. It was a strained time for all of us.

Betty got a job working at a factory in West Los Angeles, and my mom showed signs of loneliness without her good friend. One day, I saw Carolann in the hallway at school. Her mother had just dropped her off at the side door of the English building, and I don't know what possessed me to say something to her, but I said, "I wish my mother could drive me to school." It was sarcastic.

Carolann went out of the hallway and told her mom what I had said. Betty was angry with me and called the principal of the school. The principal called me to his office and asked me to apologize to Carolann. I said I would and that I was sorry for being so rude. I did apologize, but that was not the end to it. Betty met me at my front door when I returned to school. She was very angry with me and said that I should never speak to her daughter again. Mom came to the door to find out what all the shouting was about. I told Mom what

I had said and that I did apologize to Carolann. Mom said to Betty, "Then it is over. Enough said." Betty said, "You'll see, this is not over, not by any stretch of the imagination." I felt terrible, but it did get worse.

A few weeks passed. I thought it was okay now. I still didn't speak with Carolann or Betty. I didn't know what to say, and maybe just shutting up would be the best solution. My mother received a letter from the welfare department. Charges had been brought against her for hoarding clothes in the garage and also babysitting for money. Both were against the rules of the welfare department. Mom had to report for court on a weekday, and she was advised to bring counsel with her. Mom was a welfare recipient, and she stored clothes for the church missionary group in our garage. She also babysat for friends at the church, and they did pay her for caring for their children after school until they could get home from work.

The welfare money was almost gone. My sisters who were now married were no longer in the program. My brother, who was in the coast guard, was no longer in the program. It was just Trudy and me. Doris was already eighteen. The pastor of the church and many of Mom's friends went to court with her. They explained about the clothes in the garage and that the church families trusted Mom with their children and she only had them after school for a few hours. The judge said Mom was guilty of breaking the rules. He said she would now be off government assistance and needed to pay the state one dollar a month for two years to pay off the penalty.

We were not able to see who reported Mom for the violation of babysitting after school. The clothes issue was dropped. It did not matter who called the Welface office, everyone was just sad heartbroken. Mom said, God knows and God will take care of us. We didn't care about the money that would be lost to her. This money came to us because my father had died on a government project, but to lose a really good friend and her family was beyond heartbreaking, and Mom was crushed.

One month later, my mom had her first job outside the home in twenty years. She was now working for a lady at our church who owned a senior housing care center. Mom was the cook and a nurse's aide, and she loved every minute that she worked with these seniors. She got to wear a nurse's uniform, and it made her so proud to be working for a regular paycheck that she could go to a bank and cash.

The Foley family moved out of our neighborhood, and we didn't see them again until 1970. My third child, Kendra, was only a few months old, and she got pneumonia. I took her to St. John's Hospital in Santa Monica, and Linda Foley came to see me. She was working at the hospital. She heard that I was there with my baby, and she came. It was really good to see her and know that she was doing well. The next day, Carolann came to the hospital and sat with me as I sat with my baby Kendra. We talked for two hours and got caught up on their life; she also had a child.

About three weeks later, there was a knock at my front door. When I opened the door, there stood Carolann and Linda. We hugged each other, and I invited them in, but they said, "Mom is in the car. Can she come in to see you also?" "Of course," I said. "Please tell her to come in." Betty did come in, and she wrapped me in those big arms that I remembered as a child. I was glad to see her. I asked her to go see Mom, but that never happened. I never saw Betty again, and years later, I heard that she had passed away.

I will always remember the Foley family. We had ten years of great friendship with them. We had so many great memories, stories to share, school days together. We thank God for all the great times we enjoyed with our neighbors.

The Coin Collection Was Stolen

The Helms Bakery Company was located in Culver City, California. They made freshly baked goods every day and delivered them to each neighborhood. They did this with coaches, trucks, and their motto was, "Daily to your door." The driver had a whistle, and when he stopped on your street, he proudly blew that whistle, and the family members from that street would come to buy. They sold cake, pies, doughnuts, brownies, and other wonderful pastries, and we were excited if we had enough money to buy off that truck.

The coach came every day Monday through Saturday, and the purpose of course was to purchase the baked goods, but my mom had a different reason to go out to the truck. The driver and sales-person was a coin collector just like my mom, so Mom would walk out to the truck with her bag of coins and exchange that bag for a new bag of coins filled with pennies, nickels, dimes, and quarters. Every night, she would go through every coin in the bag to see if she could find just one or two special coins by date that might work its way into her collection. The driver would rotate his coins from the sale of the product, making sure the change for the company was also correct to the penny.

Mom followed this routine every day for more than ten years. When she would complete a collector's book, she would start another one, having a minimum of ten-penny books, ten-nickel books, etc., of each coin type.

When I became a teenager, it was obvious that Mom had a lot of coin books completed, and the value of those books was a lot, so we convinced her to put all the completed books into a safe-deposit box, and she would keep a lot at home to work on. She couldn't stop saving, sorting, exchanging dollar bills with people to keep the loose change in their pocket. She always had five to ten dollars' worth of change on our dining-room table. When she would find just one special coin that fit into that open slot, it was a thrill for her. She just loved it.

Mom kept bags of coins in the hall closet, bags so full that it was hard to lift them. Now she had also started to collect silver dollars, so the face value of all the coins in the closet was growing. At this time, we had no idea what the collector's value was, but many of the coins were rare, like the half dime from the 1800s.

Mom had a nephew in the military stationed somewhere in California. He wrote Mom and said he wanted to come and visit her, and would it be okay if he brought a friend with him from the same military base? Of course, everyone was welcome to come see Ellender. They arrived on the weekend. They wanted to see Santa Monica and Hollywood. Mom cooked them dinner and invited them to spend the night so they didn't have to pay for a room somewhere. Now, because he was family, she wanted to share her hobby with them. She showed them the coin collection and the hallway closet where she kept the bags of loose coins. They were amazed in the value they saw in that closet, and they went to bed thinking about all that money (they had no idea of the collector's value).

Mom was ready for church. Her ride would be picking her up anytime, so she said good-bye to the guys and asked them to shut the front door securely when they left to return to their base, never giving a second thought to leaving these two young men in her house alone. It never crossed her mind that someone whom she loved would ever hurt her.

Returning from church about 12:30 p.m., the first thing she did was go to the hall where she could change her clothes. She was shocked to find all her clothes on the floor. The coin collection was gone, the bags of coins gone. She was crying now. She was in shock. She knew instantly she should not have trusted this nephew and a total stranger in her house.

Mom called Eleanor and me, and we both came to the house immediately. We found Mom on the sofa crying. The coins were gone, and most likely, those two just spent the money, not knowing the collector's value. We consoled Mom the best we could, and on Monday morning, we called the military base where these young men were stationed, and we got a military police officer on the line. We explained what happened, gave him the two men's names, and he said he would investigate the charges.

Three days later, Mom received a call from that officer. He said they' had found the empty collector cards in the car, and the guys admitted that they took all the coins and that they had spent every last penny on food, gas, etc. They were gone forever, but the officer asked Mom if she would sign a statement of the charges, and she said yes. The two men were put into the brig (jail). They were found guilty of theft while wearing a uniform of their country, and they were given a dishonorable discharge. We never heard from them again. It was a hard lesson for Mom, and we were thankful that a large part of her collection was in a safe-deposit box and that all of her children received a completed book of pennies, nickels, dimes, quarters, and silver dollars. We also received the half dimes that were in my daddy's pocket when he died.

Mom had a lot of grandchildren, and she was working on their penny book for the next several years. She had twenty-three grandchildren at this time. She had a lot of collecting to do. My mom also collected stamps and pictures of post offices. She had twenty-five books of stamps and hundreds of pictures of United States post offices, which included airplanes and boats that delivered to remote areas of Alaska and Hawaii. I saved my coins till 2012, and when I cashed them in, I had enough money to pay for a cruise to Alaska, all expenses covered. Thank you, Mom.

Mom's First Taste of Wine

It was Mom's eightieth birthday, and my son Scott wanted to take her somewhere special for lunch. He usually bought her a hamburger from Carl's Jr., a fast-food restaurant, which was her favorite hamburger place. He would say, "Grandma, I'm coming over to visit you today. What can I bring you?" He knew before asking, but he always wanted her to tell him, "Just bring me a big hamburger from Carl's Jr., and don't forget a large Coca-Cola." Never Diet Coke, always regular Coke.

Today was special, a special year for her, and he asked her to go to Fridays restaurant in Marina del Rey. He said, "Grandma, we can sit outside on the deck and watch the boats go by in the Marina." She said, "Well, now that would just be fine." I was lucky enough to also be invited. Of course, he better not leave out his own mother, and I was happy to join them.

We arrived at the restaurant around 1:00 p.m. on Sunday afternoon, and there was room for three out on the deck, so we were seated immediately. It was a gorgeous day, warm with a soft breeze. Sure enough, the boats in the marina were on the move. Amazing how many people were on their boats on Sunday afternoon. Most were just heading out to the jetty around the large pile of rocks out beyond the breakwater. Then they would turn around and come back in, just enjoying the ride and the sun. All the other people did the same exact thing.

The waitress came over to our table to take our drink order. I ordered iced tea; Mom, a large Coke; and Scotty ordered red wine. Mom said, "What are you doing ordering wine? That stuff is terrible for you." Now, Mom was not known for being quiet, so the folks at the surrounding table heard her loud and clear and began to turn and look at us. Scott looked at me like, *Mom, what is she doing?* His eyes were huge and just staring at me. I just shrugged my shoulders and looked at the menu.

Scott took a sip of his wine and said, "Grandma, this is really good. Would you like to taste it?" "No," she said. "Why, I wouldn't have that stuff in my mouth." Scott took another taste. I was sipping my iced tea, and then out of the blue, Mom said, "Okay, give me that glass, Scott. I'll have one taste for you." She reached over and took Scott's glass. She picked up her teaspoon and dipped it into his glass and tasted the wine. "Oh no," she said, "that is so bitter. It is terrible." But she took his glass again and dipped that spoon into the wine one more time and drank it down.

By now, all the other folks around us were watching this all take place, and they were waiting anxiously for her next comment. By the third teaspoonful, Scott was looking at me again like, *Mom, what is going on here?* I was just laughing—everyone was laughing—because she didn't want to give him back his wineglass. The waitress was standing nearby, and she said to my mom, "Would you like a tablespoon?" Everyone just burst out laughing. Mom didn't see anything funny, but finally she returned Scott's wineglass, and we began to order lunch. Now, you know she ordered a big hamburger with lots of onions and another big Coke. She did make the comment that the Coke glass was very small, and they would need to fill it a lot more times.

We had a lovely lunch. She enjoyed the afternoon at Fridays, and we returned home around 4:00 p.m. We toured the marina for a while so she could see all the inlets and as many boats as possible. She had a good day, and she was tired when she got home. Maybe it was all those teaspoonfuls of wine.

A month later, I was helping Mom in her kitchen, and I opened her refrigerator, and there was a bottle of red wine on the door. "Mom, you have wine in your refrigerator?" "Well," she said, "the doctor said it might be good for my heart." I said, "Really?" "Yes," she said. "I put a little in a glass, and I sip it down with my teaspoon just like medicine. It doesn't taste so bitter that way." Really?

I later told Scott about the wine in the refrigerator. He got a great laugh out of it. He said, "I thought she was going to finish my glass that day at the restaurant."

Aunt Lois

February 2014

Now I haven't thought about my aunt Lois in many years and never really gave her a single thought. I guess the reason I am thinking about her now, is because we are going to visit cousin's in Oklahoma City. I have only seen my cousins a few times and I know this will be my last opportunity to visit with them. Steve and I have plans to travel a lot, but going over the same road a second time is not in our immediate plans. Due to our age and the bucket list we have, most likely, this will be the last time.

Obviously, I was named after this lady (Lois Smith Jones). She was my mother's best friend in the early years of my mother's life. My mother only went to school up to the eighth grade, so it is difficult to know exactly when these two women first met. As the story goes from my mother, Lois was her best friend in school. They both came from farm families, they worked the fields, and they worked taking care of the men in their house. They cooked breakfast, lunch and dinner for the men who worked the fields, cared for the animals, and fed livestock.

So, I have to start this story of where my mother met the man she was to marry. Lois Smith was dating Truman A. Jones. Lois introduced my mother (Ellender) to Emmett Jones, Truman's brother. They hung out together, not really dating, yet these men were working on formal dating with these two women. Things didn't go quite like everyone had planned, because Truman asked my mother's father (Joseph Pillars) permission to date his daughter. Whoops, Lois didn't seem so happy about the change in plans, but she soon accepted it and started to date Emmett.

Now the story goes, that Ellender married Truman and Lois married Emmett and the children started to come.

After a few years, Ellender and Truman needed to come to California and put their daughter Ima Jo in the children's polio hospital in Downey California. After a short time, Lois and Emmett decided that they should also come to California with all their kids. They found a house just down the street (Los Flores Canyon) from my parents. They put their kids on the school bus with their cousins. Life, at that point was full of hard work, babies, and trying to keep the family with food and shelter.

During this time, Doris, Lois (me) and Trudy were born. It was 1944 and my father died in the horrible cave-in under the Malibu Courthouse. This tragic accident left my mom with eight children to care for on her own.

Aunt Lois and Uncle Emmett tried to help my mother as much as possible. After all, they had five children of their own to raise, but Uncle Emmett came up to our house often. He would help my mom fix things on this old house, or kill a rattle snake or carry water up to the water tank on top of our house.

I really don't remember anything about this time. I was only four years old when my Mother decided to take the advice of the social worker and move her family to Santa Monica. In the summer of 1948; everyone in our house packed up and headed for our new home in Santa Monica, 714 Kensington Rd.

It wasn't long before Aunt Lois and Uncle Emmett followed and they bought a house in Santa Monica on Marine St. It was about a fifteen-minute drive to our house. Now is the time, I started to know who this Aunt Lois was. They came to our house on Saturday nights, and mom and Aunt Lois would cook dinner for the entire family (seven children for Ellender and five children for Lois). The older kids were high school age and they liked being cousins because they all went to Samohi (Santa Monica High School). On Saturday nights, they would all play dominoes around the dining room table. We younger kids just stayed out of their way.

One Saturday night, Aunt Lois and Uncle Emmett didn't come to our house. When we asked why, we were told to be quiet, don't ask questions. The children were to be seen but not heard, and certainly don't ask questions.

I would hear my older brother and sisters whispering about trouble going on, but I never knew the reason that they stopped coming.

Now Jo came home from Downey Rancho Los Amigos Hospital and Aunt Lois and Uncle Emmett loved Jo. That was so obvious and they loved to be around for her since we all knew that Jo would be in the wheel chair with polio for the rest of her life. However, Aunt Lois and Uncle Emmett nor the cousins ever came to see anyone, not even Jo.

When I was twelve years old I remember asking Jo; why do you think Aunt Lois and Uncle Emmett don't come to see us anymore? Jo said to me "Honey, jealousy is a horrible thing and we need to pray for our family, I hope they can make up I don't know if that will ever happen."

I still didn't understand why, but when I was sixteen, going to Samohi myself, I finally asked my mother; "whatever happen to our cousins, our aunt and uncle." She said, "Lois is a mean hateful person, very jealous of our family, and she won't ever come here again, we can never be friends again." I said, "Mom, she was your best friend, what happened." Mom said, "Lois thought that Emmett and I was having an affair and she thought that I was trying to steal her husband away from her." I replied, "Was it true?"

"Lord have mercy," she said, "I don't want that man! She can have him. Now let's stop talking about her."

Five months later, I graduated from High School and I was married to Dale. We started a life together and I really didn't think about my aunt or uncle again for years.

One day, Lou (my sister) and I were driving down Lincoln Boulevard, in Santa Monica, heading for the 3rd Street Shopping Mall. Lou said, "Look, there is Marine Street, let's go see if Aunt Lois and Uncle Emmett are still living on that street." She quickly made a right turn down the street and one block later, she said "Oh look, there they are!". They were standing in front of their house. I didn't recognize them at first, but after staring at them for a few minutes, they started to look familiar. Lou recognized them at once, since she was in high school when they came around the house.

Lou said, "Let's stop and say, hi." I replied, "okay, if you want." She stopped the car, got out, and started walking towards them. Aunt Lois starred at us for a minute and then I heard her say, "Oh my! Look who's here."

She recognized Lou, but wasn't sure who I was. Lou said, "This is Lois Maye." She grabbed me and hugged me tightly. I was a little stunned, then Uncle Emmet said, "Well Loudy, its so nice to see you and Lois, I would have never known you."

They invited us into their house and we talked for about an hour. She never mentioned my mom or Jo. She did ask about Scotty Buck, and others like Nora, Doris, and Trudy. She told us about her kids, their families, and where they all lived. As the conversation continued, I could tell she didn't like her children very much. She said, "I don't care if they ever come over here, I raised them and if they don't want to see me anymore than that is their problem." Lou then said it was time to leave. We hugged them and said our good byes. We never saw them again.

We heard they had moved to Oklahoma a few years later, they really had to move.

Aunt Lois and Betty Foley (our neighbors on Kensington road) worked together at a factory. Aunt Lois talked with Betty (who was upset with my mother as well) into reporting my mom to the Social Work department for fraud. These two women told this agency, that my mother had been caring for children illegally for extra money. This was against the welfare rules and they also said my mother was hoarding clothes in their garage. If you're receiving funds from the state, then you cannot make any extra income until you are off the welfare plan.

Of course, there was no way my mother could live on welfare with eight children. Especially, when one of them had polio. My mother received a call from one of her social workers. She explained that Aunt

Lois and Betty were looking for revenge and signed statements of witness to the fraud. My mother had to go to court. She was ordered to pay back a portion of the welfare money she received. Her attorney explained she only had to show a willingness to pay the money back. So, she paid back one dollar a month for two years. The charges for hoarding clothes for the church missionaries was dropped.

We heard gossip from the extended family in Oklahoma that many people in the family were angry with Aunt Lois. Even her own children would not speak with her. I spoke with my cousin, Joann, who was Aunt Lois's daughter. She told me they had moved to Oklahoma and they needed someone to look after them. Uncle Emmett (my father's only brother) was getting old and frail.

I know my mother really missed Aunt Lois's six children. She watched them grow up in Santa Monica and she had to say away from them to keep the peace. This was very hard on her.

Two years after the welfare incident, Trudy was the only one left at home. Mom got a job at a nearby convalescent hospital and she didn't need to iron or babysit any longer.

None of the neighbors would speak to Betty. They soon sold their house and then they were gone.

Now, I do not think my mother had an affair with Uncle Emmett, I just can't imagine that happened. He was a quiet kind of guy and rarely said two words. He smoked a lot and Aunt Lois had ran the house for sure. But, who knows, perhaps he wanted to get away from this woman. I really do not know, no one wanted anything to do with her, so that gives me some ideas that it is possible that Uncle Emmett was hoping for a better life. After all, my mother was involved in church, had a lot of friends and our house was always full of family and friends.

CHAPTER 6

How Did She Do It?

Many times through the years, relatives and friends would ask questions about Mom (Ellender Jones-Stoner), and they would say, "How did she do it? Give them clothes, food, shelter, schooling, church, medical—all the things every child needs—and do it all by herself?" Well, the answer is simple: she didn't do it alone. She had a lot of help.

Rancho Los Amigos Hospital

This was a place for Jo to live and get the care she needed as a polio patient. No way could Mom had given her the medical care, surgery, iron lung and kept her alive without the help of the doctors and nurses. Jo would have died. The doctors in Oklahoma told Mom to take Jo to California. She could get the help that Jo needed there. Mom and Dad did what they had to do, and they went to California.

The Pippenberg Family

Mr. and Mrs. Pippenberg gave Mom and Dad a place to live. They gave them jobs to earn a living. They gave them hope for the children who would be born in California. The Pippenbergs lived in Malibu, California. They owned two houses in Los Flores Canyon. As I understand it, they charged very little for rent in the early '40s.

It was the end of the war. The houses were not insulated, just wood slates, but Mom and Dad were happy to have a place to live.

Welfare Department of California

After my father died, Mom needed help with her eight children, and the California Welfare Department was there to help. Were they strict? Yes. Were the counselors mean? Yes, they were, but Mom needed help to support her children. She only had an eighth grade education. She had seven children and one on the way when my father was killed, so she did what needed to be done and obeyed the rules. Each child was given a little money for support until they were eighteen years old. When the social worker came, everyone was on their best behavior. The first social worker was the best. She helped Mom get a house in Santa Monica that was close to schools, shopping, and medical help if needed. Mom purchased her house on Kensington Street for twelve thousand dollars, and she put five hundred dollars down. Five hundred dollars was all the money she was able to save in the last five years.

My Older Sisters

Marge, Lou, and Nora were already teenagers and able to work, so after school, they got jobs and brought their paychecks home to Mom. This was the only way Mom could feed and house everyone and keep Jo in the hospital.

Everyone had to help. I mean, all the brothers and sisters helped in the yard and housework. There were always ironing, washing dishes, washing clothes, and cooking to be done every day. There were beds to be made, furniture to be dusted, windows to be washed, and the dog to be fed. Every child did their share of work every day.

Mom stood at the ironing board from 6:00 a.m. to 10:00 p.m. every day but Sunday. She did laundry for people at church or in the neighborhood to keep money coming in. On Monday, folks dropped off their laundry; and Friday, they would pick it up. Every Friday, we had clothes hanging in every doorway, every curtain rod, on the front door, just everywhere; and then on Saturdays, she would iron our clothes for Sunday church. On Sunday, Mom would rest after church. Sometimes she would take a nap, but most the time, you would see her cooking the next meal at the stove. The pots would be boiling with soup, chili, gravy, always something for the next meal.

Our Neighbors

We had great neighbors for many years. They would help take kids to school on a rainy day and drive my siblings to and from school so they wouldn't be late for work. They helped drive us to the dentist or doctor when needed, and then there were very special people who picked us up and drove us to church every Sunday, never missing a time. And if they needed to be away on a weekend, they would arrange rides for us. This went on for more than fifteen years. Dick Scheidt, Bob Kays, Bob Woods, Mrs. Hungate, Sally Miller—so many wonderful, giving people.

Our Church, Centinela Avenue
Southern Baptist Church of West Los Angeles

The people in this church loved my mom, and she loved them back. Many times, I remember hearing my mom crying in the hallway or bathroom late at night. She would be on the phone with the church pastor, telling them that she couldn't pay the water bill this month, or maybe it was a letter in her hand saying they would cut off our electricity next Monday. So many times, we could barely pay our way, but the church always came through for us. They would pay that bill, and when Mom received her check from the state, she would pay the church back. They were the first on her list. She was heartbroken that she couldn't pay her 10 percent tithe like the Bible asked for. She wanted to pay so badly, but there just wasn't enough money from the babysitting and ironing to pay all the bills. Our family cleaned the church on Saturdays, no pay, and this was her way of paying God for all the many blessings. We did this for ten years. She took care of the nursery during church time so the children were well taken care of.

She taught Sunday school classes and sang in the choir. She mended people's clothes for free to make sure she was doing her fair share. Everyone knew that Ellender was giving her fair share.

The Salvation Army

They were great, wonderful people who came every Thanksgiving and Christmas and gave us turkey, cranberry sauce, gravy, corn bread, and always at Christmas, a small gift for each child. One year, I received a handmade clown doll. I just loved this doll, and I still have it today, sixty-five years later. I will keep it till the day I die. Maybe I will be buried with it. It gives me a lot of wonderful memories just to have it close by.

Mom was grateful and would give all the folks who stopped by a big thank-you individually. She would give them some iced tea and make them feel special. We certainly felt special by the generosity of the Salvation Army.

Fire Department and Police Department

A fireman or policeman would stop by often to check on us. They would look at the fireplace and make sure it was safe. They called my mom the widow woman of Santa Monica or her nickname *Jonesy*, which was given to her by the neighbors. They also brought small gifts for Christmas like school supplies, canned goods, or gift certificates. Everything was a gift of love, and we all appreciated their kindness, even though I was scared of them. After all, they were men in uniforms, and that was scary enough for me. I would usually hide behind my mom, and no way I would talk to them.

Butter Is on Sale at the Market

It seems silly, but butter was very needed. Mom cooked everything in lard or butter, and when a coupon for butter would appear in the *Evening Outlook* paper, Mom would get all the coupons from the neighbors' paper and give each of her children fifty cents to go to the market and buy a pound of butter. That meant we got eight pounds of butter that week, and Mom was happy about that. We would collect pop bottles in the alley and save them until we had enough change to go buy my sister Jo an orange pop. She loved them, and it was a rare treat for her to have one. It took the refund of twenty Coke bottles to buy that drink for her. That must've cost maybe forty or fifty cents for that orange pop.

Mrs. Deichman

This lady was Jo's home teacher provided by the state, but she was more than just a teacher. She was a gift from God. She spent a lot of hours with Jo so that she could graduate from Santa Monica High School. Jo didn't get any schooling at the hospital, so she had a lot of catching up to do. Mrs. Deichman didn't get paid for all the hours she spent at our house. She loved Jo, and she wanted her to succeed. Mrs. Deichman was like a member of our family. She ate meals with us, and Mom would make her coffee. This was special because we were not allowed coffee in our house. The church said it was bad for you, so forget it.

Mrs. Deichman went to my sisters' weddings. She came to parties, bridal showers, etc. Like before, she was a wonderful, loving woman who really cared about Jo and our family.

So, as you see, Mom had a lot of help. There was never a dull moment in our house. There were always people coming and going, everyone extending a hand. But I don't want to forget about two more people.

Our Doctor

He always came to the house. He knew Mom didn't drive, and when he needed to give medical care to us, he would stop by at night.

Pastor Lloyd Miller

He drove Mom wherever she needed to go. One night, it was very late, and Mom got sick, really doubling up in pain. Pastor Miller came and picked her up, drove her to the general hospital in Los

Angeles, and sat with her all night. It turned out she had a twisted bowel. She needed surgery, and he saved her life according to the doctors. What a great man he was, so caring and so giving. He loved my mom and our family; he was another gift from God.

We could not have grown up in a better place than Santa Monica, California, just the perfect place for our family. God knew what was best for our family. He always answered our prayers and was always faithful.

Ellender — July 19, 1997
88 years old

Grandchildren

Great Grandchildren

Ellender's Bible

Her Bible sat on the coffee table in the living room. She read scripture every evening and with prayer for her children, her church. She prayed constantly for another day of electricity, another day of water and gas, and just to be able to pay her bills. She would say to us kids, "By the grace of God, we can face another day."

She carried her Bible to church every Wednesday night for prayer meeting. She carried it to church on Sunday for both the 9:00 a.m. service and again for the 5:00 p.m. service. She never failed to do this. She wrote in her Bible, underlining scripture that she wanted to remember. She wrote in the margins of each page, writing the date and the pastor's name who preached using that scripture on that Sunday.

Dick Schleidt had given Mom this Bible in the early '50s. He had her name written in gold lettering on the front. She loved Dick, and she loved this Bible. Dick was about thirty years old, and he went to our church. He became friends with our family, and he drove us to church, both Wednesday nights and Sundays, never failing to show up for more than five years. By the '90s, this Bible of hers was showing a lot of wear. The back was coming apart, and she taped it together. I thought it was time for her to have a new Bible, and I gave her a New King James Bible with large lettering on December 24, 1996. She liked my Bible, but she still carried her old faithful Bible to church every Sunday. One of her most favorite verse was Proverbs 3:5–6.

When mom found out that she had cancer, she was eighty-eight years old. She said, "Well, this is just fine. I have been praying to my God for eighty-eight years, and now I finally get to see him. Bring me my Bible. I have some reading to do." No, not the new Bible that I gave her in 1996, she wanted the old tattered Bible that had been her friend for so many years, the one that had been written on so many times that you could hardly read the scripture for all the ink marks. She said, "This Bible feels good in my hands, just like a good friend. It feels safe and secure."

This old Bible sat on the nightstand right next to her hospital bed. It was her most trusted gift. Every word was a gift from God to love and accept, not because she earned it but a gift freely given from her precious Lord Jesus who had died for her. Ellender died at the age of eighty-nine.

CELEBRATION OF LIFE

Mary Ellender Pillars Jones Stoner

Child, wife, mother, grandmother,
great grandmother, great-great grandmother

World's Greatest Mother

There's a special place where great mothers are kept.
It's in the hearts of their children, the people for whom
mom's have given their souls, they've loved and forgiven.
So, mother, to you we've been grateful for all that you've shared—
your patience and kindness, humor and grace—
You're a mom beyond compare.

My Mother's Hands

July 1998

My mother was preparing to meet her Father in heaven. The doctors said it would only be a few months, maybe days. I realized that I needed help, permanent help, with Mom. I had lived with my mom, Ellender Stoner, for two months; and every day I saw changes, changes that told me that Mom needed a full-time caretaker. My salary at Home Depot was sufficient to care for all the material things we needed, but I could not leave her alone. I needed to call Marge and convince her to come and live with us. She could take care of Mom, and I could continue to work.

Marge was my oldest sister. She lived in Laughlin, and she agreed to come, for which I was so grateful. I believed we could use this time together to take care of Mom and heal the emotional scars that had consumed our lives this past year, me from divorce and Marge from losing her beloved Jack, her husband of forty-eight years. And Mom, she was facing her fear of death. I believed that God brought us together for a reason, and he would give us the time to heal through this crisis.

August

Marge and I had spent many hours in these two months sharing stories, remembering when we were young, remembering the first time we went to church together at the Centinela Baptist Church in West Los Angeles. We tried to count all the jobs my mom held at this church over the twenty-five years she attended: she taught Sunday school and Vacation Bible School, cleaned the church every Saturday morning, attended every Wednesday night prayer meeting, sang in the choir for at least fifteen years, was in charge of the nursery care, attended women's missionary ministries, cooked a Sunday meal for all visiting pastors and their families, and won Mother of the Year three times. And she won three Bibles for being the mom with the most children every Mother's Day.

Late August, Thursday evening

Doris, my sister who was one year older than me, came every day after work to see Mom and give us that extra support we needed daily. Trudy, my sister who was one year younger than me, was coming tomorrow. She had bought Mom a new bathrobe and pajamas. This would be great. Mom needed some clean bedding; it was difficult to keep up with the laundry. Lou and Nora, also sisters who were older than me, would be here on Friday and stay the weekend. Nora gave Mom the spiritual guidance that she needed, and Lou took care of all of us with meals and cleanup.

Jo and Tom, my sister from Denver and her husband, would also arrive this weekend, thank God. Mom would be so glad to see them. We were praying that everyone would be here before Mom left us. Scotty Buck, my only brother, would arrive on Sunday from Florida. It was going to be so hard for him. We girls had been with Mom on a daily basis and had seen her body melt away slowly, but Buck had not seen her since her birthday in July, so he would be shocked at how her body had changed. Mom was still conscious and was able to speak with us. She was not in any pain. She slept a lot now and ate very little. Marge and the hospice home-care nurse saw to her bath, keeping her as comfortable as possible.

Saturday morning

Jo and Tom arrived. How wonderful to have them here. We all needed them, their support, their prayers; and of course, Mom wanted to talk with them for as long as possible. Jo looked amazingly strong, but Tom was very tired from the long drive from Denver. He needed a hot shower and a good meal, and he could go to sleep while Jo sat with Mom for as long as Jo could sit up in her wheelchair.

Saturday afternoon

Lou, Nora, Doris, Trudy, Jo, Marge, and I were all sitting around Mom's hospital bed. We had decided to keep her at home (on Carmelina Street; this was her home in West LA). She did not want to go to a hospital. We girls could take care of her. Jo began to sing, and I heard the sweet sound and words and music: I came to the garden alone while the dew was still on the roses, and the voice I hear fell on my ear. This voice was calling to me. He walked with me, and he talked with me, and he told me I am his own. The joy we shared as we stood there teary-eyed, no other will ever know.

Lois continued to sing with, "Precious Lord, take my hand, lead me on, let me stand. I am tired, I am weak, I am worn. Through the storm of the night, lead me on to the light. Take my hand, Precious Lord, lead me home." (The words of this song came from our church hymnal.) How we all loved to sing our favorite gospel songs around the piano in our home on Kensington in Santa Monica. Jo or Marge would play the piano on Sundays, and we would all gather around the piano and harmonize the music, which became such a huge part of our lives.

> Every day with Jesus is sweeter than the day before
> Every day with Jesus, I love him more and more
> Jesus saves and keeps me and he's the one I waited for
> Every day with Jesus is sweeter than the day before[1]

We must have sung for a solid hour, harmonizing just like we did forty years ago. I don't remember when we stopped singing. It just became very quiet as we all just sat and thought about our youth, our home, growing up with Mom, and the impact that she had on each of our lives. Now we waited, waited for the angels to come for her. Our Lord would be calling her name very soon.

Sunday morning

Scotty Buck arrived. We were all here at home at last. As he walked in, we all stopped breathing. The emotion of this moment was overwhelming. Everyone was crying, hugging, kissing, and praising God because we knew, at this very moment, that we could get through

---

1   Lois Lingard. Words from the song are from the *Worship and Service Hymnal* published in 1968.

this. We were all together at last, all eight of us. We could hold one another, praising God, when we were up and hold one another when we were sad.

Through the days to follow, we all had our one-on-one with Mom, saying our good-byes, thanking her for the years of love and hard work to keep this family together for more than fifty-five years. She would be leaving us all with such great memories and great love and respect for our siblings—knowing that because of her total dedication to all of us, we would always be strong, always take care of one another. Of course, we would miss her so much, but we knew that she would be preparing for us to come to heaven, and we would see her again.

Many, many family and friends came daily to say their good-byes, laughing and talking about the special times they had spent with this special woman, mom, and grandmother. Mom was awake and able to hug and say good-bye to everyone whom she wanted to see. I stopped counting at over one hundred people. Many came day after day, encouraging the family and bringing food, gifts, and of course, their prayers. The grandchildren came, sitting by her bed, holding her hands, telling her how much they loved her. She had sixty-nine grandchildren, twenty-three grandchildren, and forty-six great-grandchildren, ranging from one year to about thirty-five years of age.

I need to mention my dog Bucky (lovingly named after my brother), an overfed cocker spaniel that mom and I both loved. Bucky would sleep under Mom's hospital bed, and he rarely left this spot. Mom could just drop her hand down by the side of the bed, and Bucky would lick it and whine a little. He knew Mom would be leaving us soon.

Now, saying all this brings me to the hour I sat with Mom alone. She slept the entire time. It was early morning. I couldn't sleep, and I just wanted to sit by her bed and hold her hand. I found myself holding her rough right hand, stroking her thick skin, which still showed signs of calluses on her palm from the years of hard work ironing clothes year after year to support this family. Her fingers had knotted, and her joints twisted from the years of arthritis.

As I recalled these incredible life-sharing years, I looked down, deep down, into the hands. I wanted to remember every detail of the life of the woman (my mom) who was slipping away from us.

At eighty-nine years old, she had grown up as a farmer's daughter, really working hard from early morning till late at night. She married at nineteen and was picking cotton and moving from farm to farm, trying to keep her children fed. She had lost one child to polio (Inez). She had lost one baby at eighteen days (Allie June). No one knows the real reason why this baby died. "Breathing disorder," said the doctor. Then she had Ima Jo in the hospital as a polio patient in Los Angeles. Ellender lost her husband, our father, to a tragic accidental death in May 1944. Mom continued to cook, clean, wash and iron, and babysit from sunup to sunset. These hands had raised eight children. She watched each of these children grow to maturity, and then the grandchildren started coming and coming and coming. Right at this time, Mom had sixty-nine grandchildren.

Mom's hands not only picked cotton and ironed but also grew a garden, harvesting her own fruits and vegetables, raising chickens, killing and cleaning them and frying them up for our dinner. She canned all her own food for the long winter months. She made a lot of our clothes, cutting the pattern out of used newspapers. She worked at the church, served meals to the homeless, made dinner every Sunday for friends and family. She crocheted bandages for a missionary project and made each of her grandchildren three afghans for their high school graduation. She collected stamps and coins and traveled the States to be part of the coin conventions. She took pictures of post offices, thousands of them, and kept them safe for the post office museum in Arkansas. These were the hands that grew her own flowers, pruned her roses, and took them to the church for Sunday service.

Mom never had a manicure. Her hands were rough and course. She had split cuticles and scars from cuts and injuries from who knows when. I looked deep into that hand I was holding and remembered her strength and the tests that she had to endure. These hands had held songbooks and, for hours upon hours, held her Bible, studying the words that the Lord had given to her. She would underline scripture that was meaningful to her. Her Bible was almost entirely underlined. We had her Bible sitting on her nightstand. If she woke, she would want it.

My mom had cooled these hands in the Jordan River and washed these hands in the Sea of Galilee as she strolled along the beach. She toured the Holy Land with friends from her church. She told me that she didn't know that touching water could be such a living, changing experience.

Mom had a firm, solid handshake. She extended this hand to all members and visitors of the First Baptist Church of WLA for more than fifteen years. She said, "There's nothing better than the feeling of spiritual contact with other Christians joining together to worship on a Sunday morning."

I studied these hands for several days. I wanted to remember every story, every detail, of her life. The joy, laughter, tears, fears, excitement, and I could only wonder, would my hands tell the same story to my children?

It was early in the morning now, about 6:00 a.m., and again, I just wanted to sit by her bedside and hold her hand. My mother was dying from pancreatic cancer. Her body was slowly melting away. By now, she was only taking a little water, and her hands felt cold. I took some lotion and began to massage her hands, rubbing them until I could feel them warning up again. I felt a little squeeze back from her. She was still with us even though she said very little now. Once again, I could hear Jo and Lou humming a gospel song, and I could see Mom's finger tapping along with the rhythm of the music.

August 28, 1998

Mom had slipped into a coma. All my sisters, brother, and brothers-in-law (Tom and George) had taken their turns sitting with Mom today. We know her time was near, and we needed to say our last good-bye. Nora said, "I hope I get to see the angels come for her." It was such a warm day. We had the fans going and the windows open. Glasses of iced tea were everywhere, and the girls continued to sing throughout the day. The hospice nurse came. She took care of Mom, and she gave us all a hug good-bye. She knew that she would not be needed again. Marge asked her to please come to the funeral. She said she would. We thanked God for this angel of mercy.

At 11:52 p.m., I heard Bucky, my dog, whining. He began to move around under Mom's hospital bed. He ran to the front door and then back under Mom's bed. I said, "Bucky, what is the matter?" I had been resting on the sofa only two feet away. Then again, he ran to the front door, whining. The door was open, so we could feel the cool air. Nora was asleep in the chair. I turned to Mom and could see she was gone. She was not breathing. The angels had come for her, and Bucky was the only one who saw them. Nora woke up, and she said, "Oh! Bucky saw the angels. I had hoped I would see them." Everyone was now awake. The only thing to do now was cry and thank God for having spent our lives with this incredible woman.

My mother taught us to live, and she taught us to die: just stay focused on your Heavenly Father.

The Last Tribute to a Woman of Courage

Jo and Tom were still with us in West Los Angeles. They had driven out from Denver, Colorado. Scotty Buck was here. He had come from Fort Lauderdale to be with Mom. All of us together, all eight of Ellender's children, made the last decisions concerning our mother and her last service at church.

The pastor was contacted. The mortuary staff couldn't be nicer or more helpful, so with all the input, taking everyone into consideration, travel times were set, flowers were ordered, and a bulletin written and edited about Mom's life and her family. Everything was laid out for everyone to see. The date for the funeral was set for the following Thursday.

Jo took Mom's address book and started calling every person in the book, telling them that Mom had passed and the funeral would be next week on Thursday. Flowers began to arrive that very evening. Friends and family stopped by with food, just wanting to know what they could do to help.

The week went so fast. Thursday morning came, and everything was ready. Family members started arriving at the church. We had set up ropes in the aisles to save the front seats for the family. We set up tables in the foyer to display Mom's stamp-collection books, her coin collection, and afghans that she had crocheted for her grandchildren to be given to them on their high school graduation day. In the sanctuary, ten rows on both sides of the aisle were family members. I had really not thought that so many could come. Nieces, nephews, uncles, aunts, sisters, my brother and his wife (Judy), grandchildren, and great-grandchildren were all in attendance, so there was only standing room in the sanctuary. The pastor got up and said to everyone, "Please move as closely as possible to each other." So many of our church members would like to come in for the service; everyone was adjusting their seats.

Mom's casket was brought in by the pallbearers. My heart was breaking, and I knew I must stay strong for my children. Several pastors and choir leaders spoke about Ellender's love for her Lord and Savior. They told about her personal life raising eight children by herself, with help from the church, of course. They told about her being Mother of the Year voted by the church congregation. They mentioned all the years she volunteered in the choir, the nursery, the women's missionary society. A friend of Trudy's sang two beautiful hymns, and my sister Nora got up to speak on behalf of the family. She read a long list of names of friends who have been so kind to our family, bringing food and sitting with Mom for hours on end. For their prayers, the love, and all the hugs, she called out each person by name; they had given of themselves so graciously during Mom's six months of cancer. She thanked the doctors who came to the house and who were so kind, praying with the family and with Mom, giving us instructions for her care each step of the way. Nora thanked the church and the pastors for their love over all the years for Mom and just giving the support she needed to get her children raised and married. This was her wish in life, that all her children marry and have a lot of grandchildren for her.

Ellender's grandsons served as her pallbearers. Her casket was placed in the back of the hearse. The cars began to line up behind, and over fifty cars were ready for the long trip from West Los Angeles to the Chatsworth Cemetery. Two officers on motorcycles led the way, clearing the traffic; there were no stops all the way. Family and friends gathered around the spot where Mom's body lay next to her husband, Ed Stoner Sr. She loved this spot and made sure that this was the place where she wanted to rest her bones.

The pastor, Van Elliott, a personal friend for so many years, gave the grave-site eulogy. Two hundred balloons were given out to all family and friends. The bagpiper played "Amazing Grace." The family stood and said, "We love you, Mom," and we released the balloons to heaven. We stood and watched them drift upward until there was only a small speck in the sky.

A lot of hugging, crying, and kissing continued for several minutes, and then it was time to go. Our final good-bye was done, and we had finished the eighty-nine years of Mom's life. We had completed all her wishes, her hopes, her dreams. Now it was left of to each one of us individually to live the life that our mother would want and prayed for each of us.

Jo and Tom left for Denver the next morning. Buck would be on a plane to Fort Lauderdale in the week to come. Many of us just sat around the house for a few more days, just remembering, finding closure, mourning the passing of an amazing woman, a child of God who served her time on this earth with great courage.

The angels carried Mom's soul right into heaven. We all knew that there was great rejoicing from the heavenly choir as she entered those golden gates. When she saw Jesus, we know he said to her, "Good work, my faithful servant."

Bucky our dog

Bucky (My Precious Dog)

1996

I was working for Home Depot in the Marina del Rey store. It was a really busy day, with customers swarming the store, and I was happy to finally get a break. I decided to go out front, sit on a bench, and just catch my breath. As I sat quietly, I noticed that there was a large group of people gathered in front of the store toward the opposite end to where I was sitting. I walked down in that direction to see what was going on, and immediately I could see dogs and cats, cages of all sizes, and people playing with puppies. There was a sign that said "Pet Rescue Today." I just love dogs, but now that I lived alone, the last thing I needed was a pet to care for. But I couldn't resist.

I picked up one of the puppies and cuddled her in my arms. She was adorable, and I was instantly in love with every puppy. I put her down and started back toward my bench. Then I saw this little cocker dog in a cage. It was a dirty little thing, curled up and looking very lonely. I just had to ask, "So why isn't this dog out with the others?" The lady said to me, "He is a rescue dog. He was hit by a car, broke his back leg, and needed to have surgery." Looking closer, I could see the stitches across his back hip. All the hair had been shaved off, but you could see tire marks on his back and side. I said, "So what happens to him now?" She said, "He had tags on when we found him. The owner was notified, and the owner said, 'The dog is damaged. I don't want him anymore. Do whatever you want with him.'" I was shocked. How could anyone not care for their pet? I reached inside the cage and began to touch his dirty little head. He licked my fingers, and my heart sank. Once again, the lady said to me, "Could you take him home and care for him, just till his leg heals? Then you can bring him back to the shelter for someone to adopt." I said, "I have to go back to work. I have four more hours on the clock." "No problem," she said. "We will be out here till five, and you can pick him up then. The cage can go with him for him to sleep in." "Okay, I'll be here at five to pick him up."

I drove home. The dog didn't move, bark, or whimper. He just lay still. The one thing they said to me was that the stitches had to remain dry for them to heal, so I needed to carry him outside to go pee and do his business then carry him back into the house. This dog smelled terrible. He was dirty, oily, his hair all matted down. He was the saddest little thing you've ever seen. I washed his face. I could see he was a cocker, probably a mixed breed. I fed him and gave him a warm blanket, and he curled up and slept all night. I had the next day off, so I spent the day just caring for this sad little thing, and he started to perk up a little by the third day. I couldn't stand the smell another minute, so it was time for a shower with a lot of soap. I covered his stitches the best that I could, put him in my shower, and began the warm water. He didn't move. He just looked at me like he was saying, *Finally, thank you.*

After drying him with a towel and a blow-dryer, I couldn't stop looking at him. He was beautiful. His fur and markings were great. He was adorable and so loveable, and he didn't give me a minute of problem. Even when I went to work, he had a clean blanket, water, food, and a radio turned on very low to keep him company. I couldn't wait to get home and play with him. No way was this dog going to a shelter. I was hooked, and he needed a name. I would call him Bucky. This was my brother's name. My brother loved dogs and was always bringing home a stray, so his name was now Bucky.

Bucky was a great pet, a friend, a joy to have around. He made my life a lot less lonely, and I could talk to him about anything. He seem to understand everything I would say. He just gave me kisses, and I knew it was going to be just fine.

It was time for me to sell my house. My mother was very ill. She had cancer, and I made the decision to sell my house, put all my things to storage, and go live in my mother's house so that I could care for her. "Mom," I said, "I need to come live with you. You need care, and as this cancer progresses, you will need a lot more care, and I am bringing Bucky with me." She said, "I don't want any dang old dog in my house. He will have to stay outside." Mom had a cat, and that cat lived inside the house. I said, "I will take care of the dog, and he will have a nice place to sleep in the garage if that is what you want." "Okay," she said, "you can move in."

I set up the guest bedroom for me, and I continued to work at Home Depot, caring for Mom, the dog, and the cat. Mom would sit outside on her lawn swing, and she would pet Bucky on his head. He loved just sitting with her, licking her fingers. On the fourth day, it was raining outside. She said, "Bring Bucky in the house. He will catch his death of cold out there." From the time on, Bucky lived in the house and slept in my room with me. Mom had her cat, and we made it work.

Mom was getting worse; I needed help with her. She could no longer stay alone. My sister Marge came to live with us. Mom was now in a hospital bed in the living room. Bucky stayed under her bed all the time. He only went outside to do his business and ran back into the house and went back under her bed. I tried to move him to a different spot, but he wouldn't have it. He just ran under her bed. I noticed soon that she was dropping her hand by the side of the bed, and he would lick her fingers. She would say, "Good boy,

Bucky, good boy." For the next two months, this dog never left her side. He would only eat his food under her bed. Neighbors, friends, and family who came to sit with Mom couldn't believe the devotion this dog had to her. Mom would just smile and say, "He knows. He knows my time to go is close."

It was now August 25, 1998. All the family was at the house, and Mom was in a coma. We knew that she would not be with us much longer. We all took turns sitting with Mom, and this little dog was right in the middle of everything, standing between me and the bed, looking at me, then looking at Mom, then back at me again. This dog was really restless.

It was a very warm night at 10:00 p.m. The front door was open, and the screen door was locked. My brother and sisters were all sitting around Mom's bed. Some were napping; some were talking softly. It was my turn to sit by Mom's side. I was holding her hand, just saying a prayer that the angels would come and take Mom home, her heavenly home. She was ready to go. Just at the moment, the dog stood up, looked at me, looked at Mom, and ran to the screen door. I said, "It is okay, baby. No one is out there." "Ruff," he barked quietly. He ran back under the bed, and I heard him whining. I walked to the door and put the porch light on. No one was there. I went back to my chair and looked over at Mom as she took her last breath. She was gone, and this little dog saw the angels come for her. He came from out under her bed and put his paws upon the side of the bed, just as if he was saying good-bye. My sister Nora woke up and said, "Bucky saw the angels come for Mom. He has stood watch over her for months for just this moment."

I now had to move to Corona to live near my daughter. My new house would not be ready for two months, so there was no place for Bucky to stay. I would not put him in a kennel or shelter, no way.

The man who lived next door to my mom ended up buying my mom's house for his mother to live in. "There is just one more thing. I want Bucky to stay here with my mom. She loves dogs, and I told her how Bucky took care of your mom," he said. After a lot of prayer, I said, "Yes, Bucky could stay with you." He was a good man, a good neighbor, and I knew Bucky would be safe and happy there.

A year later, I stopped by my mom's old house to just see if Bucky would remember me. The lady at the door said, "I am so sorry, little Bucky died. We found him curled up under the lawn swing in the backyard."

So now Bucky and Mom are sharing heaven together.

CHAPTER 7

The Angel Appeared by Jo

1998

This is a story that was told to me late on the evening of August 1998. My sister Jo and I were sitting with Mom. Mom was very ill with pancreatic cancer, and my sisters were all here at my mother's house. We had been taking turns sitting with Mom, holding her hand and reassuring her that we are always with her.

Jo and I had been up all day. We were so tired. I had worked my usual shift at Home Depot. I put in my eight hours, and Jo and Marge, along with my brother-in-law Tom, Jo's husband, had been with Mom while I was gone. After dinner, the dishes were cleared, and Marge told me to just sit with Mom. She would wash the dishes; then she would like to go to sleep. It had been an exhausting day for her also.

Tom went outside to smoke his pipe. He liked to sit out on the front porch and breathe in the smoke from his pipe and enjoy the cool night air. Jo wheeled herself over to the foot of Mom's hospital bed and put her hand on Mom's feet. She looked at me and said, "Lois, Mom's feet are still warm." I smiled, sat down beside Mom, and picked up her right hand. The doctor told us earlier that day that when the end got close, the first sign was that her feet would get cold.

I began to hum "Amazing Grace" just softly in my head. I was remembering the words:

Amazing grace, how sweet the sounds
that saved a wretch like me
I once was lost, but now I am found
Was blind but now I see

I thought for a moment that no one could hear me. I thought that it was so soft only I knew I was humming, but soon Jo began to sing the first chorus with me, just softly, saying the words out loud:

Amazing grace, how sweet the sound
that saved a wretch like me
I once was lost, but now I am found
Was blind but now I see

It was just like we used to do when we were kids. All the sisters liked to harmonize our church songs before we left for church on Sunday mornings, but we had lived apart, now in different states. It had been years since we had sung together. I hadn't forgotten the words. We got through three choruses and just looked at one another and smiled. The tears began to flow. So many years had passed, and so many babies had been born. Where had the time gone? And all knew that Mom would be going home to heaven very soon.

Marge turned out the lights in the kitchen, walked down the hall, and we heard the door close. She had finally gotten to bed and was asleep before her head hit the pillow. Jo said to me, "Lois, I've been thinking about a story I would like to share with you. It's about me and what happened to me a few years ago. I have only shared this story with a couple of people because I was not sure anyone would believe me. But Lo"—she sometimes called me Lo—"I think you will believe me. It's a true story."

"Do you remember when Tom was in the hospital the last time in 1985? Or about the doctors telling me that Tom's cancer had returned to his throat? His throat had collapsed, and they had to put in a breathing tube. This endoscope, flexible tube, would be permanent. He would not be able to breathe without it. They said that Tom needed to stop smoking the pipe immediately. But not only that. The cancer could have spread, and his larynx and tongue would eventually have to be removed. The last words the doctor said to me was, 'I have no idea how long he can live in this condition.'"

Jo continued, "I called the pastor of our church and asked him to call all our friends and to hold a prayer vigil in the lobby of the hospital. Within an hour, thirty or forty people had come, knelt down in the lobby of the hospital, and began to pray for Tom's recovery."

They had prayed for several hours when Jo's neighbor and good friend stopped at the hospital to see what he could do to help. Jo asked him to take her home. She had sat in her wheelchair for more than twenty-four hours; she needed to go home and lie down on her water bed. My sister Jo had polio. She had lived her life in a wheelchair since she was three years old.

This friend took her home, lifted her out of her chair, and laid her down on her bed and helped her to be as comfortable as possible. He said to Jo, "What else can I do for you? I will come back first thing tomorrow and put you back in your chair. I'll have my wife come and help you get dressed."

Jo thanked the man and just closed her eyes. She said her eyes were so swollen from crying all day that just to close them caused her whole face to hurt. They felt so heavy and sore. Once more, she began to cry. Having polio and paralyzed, she could not move. She could not go wash her face or even reach for a tissue. She pulled the sheet up to her face and used it to wipe off her face. She didn't want to open her eyes again, but for an instant, she saw a bright light. As she opened her eyes more, she could see a much brighter light, but her eyes were not hurting. She could see plainly. She looked upward, and there in the corner of her bedroom was a beautiful angel. The angel reached out her hand and spoke softly, gently, "Jo, stop crying. God has sent me with a message for you." Jo told me, "I could not speak. I was totally relaxed, breathing calmly. I was just looking at her with amazement. "The angel was in a white robe, had long hair, but with no wings. There was just a lovely yellow, pink, and blue glow around her. The angel began to speak again. She smiled and said, 'Tom is not going to die. It's not his time. God knows you need him. God has heard the prayers of his people. Stop crying. Go to sleep and know that God is with you.'" And she was gone. Jo shut her eyes, took a deep breath, and went into a sound sleep. The next thing she remembered was her neighbor, her friend, touching her shoulder and saying, "Morning, Jo, would you like some breakfast?" Jo remembered the angel and the angel's message. She was totally rested, and her friend helped her get dressed. The husband came in and lifted Jo back into her wheelchair. The three of them enjoyed breakfast together and headed back to the hospital. Jo was anxious to share this good news with Tom.

Tom did recover. He learned how to use the breathing tube. In just a few short weeks, he returned to work and never stopped smoking that pipe. Yes, the smoke came out through the hole in his neck, unless he used a cloth to cover the hole; then it came out of his mouth. He never lost his voice or his tongue, and the cancer did not come back.

Jo finished her story and just smiled at me. I had tears running down my face. Yes, I believe the story that Jo told me. I had never known her to lie about anything. I had always seen the love of Jesus Christ through this sister of mine. I am so blessed to have grown up with her, to love her, to sing with her. She was truly a blessing to all who knew her. And she saw and heard the voice of a real angel from heaven.

Jo died in October 1999. Polio finally had taken its toll. She was sixty-five years old. I was so blessed to be standing by her bed and singing "Amazing Grace" when she took her last breath.

Tom died in 2001.

Irma Jo

Time to Say Good-bye to Jo

Doris and I were living in my house in Corona, California, a small three-bedroom house that I bought after Mom had died. I needed a place to live when Mom's house had to be sold. It was my brother's property in the WLA area. I decided that Corona was close to my daughter Terri, and so I purchased this new model home and asked Doris to come and live with me for a while. I was working at Home Depot in Corona, managing the carpet department. On this particular evening, Doris and I had been waiting for a call from Denver, Colorado. My niece Dorothy Jo was to call us with an update on my sister Jo's condition.

Jo had been ill for some time. She had been in and out of the hospital in Denver several times during the last few months. She had gone through surgery, a colostomy, and her kidneys were shutting down. They had hoped that the colostomy would help her condition, but the polio in her body was back in great force, and she was in so much pain. Jo had polio since she was three years old; Jo was born in 1934. The doctors had told my mom that Jo would probably live till she was about twenty-one, but they were not sure of anything. While living at Rancho Los Amigos hospital in Downey, California, a hospital for polio patients, she had endured an iron-lung machine and twenty-seven surgeries. She lived at that hospital from about 1940 until she was able to live at home again in 1950.

It was 9:00 p.m. We were about to go to bed thinking that no news was good news. I was turning down my bedspread to crawl under the covers when the phone rang. I answered it immediately, and it was Dorothy. "Aunt Lois," she said, "Mom is worse. She doesn't look good to me, and they're just barely managing her pain." "Okay, honey, what would you like us to do for you?" "Aunt Lois," she said, "you better come right away, or you may not get to say good-bye." I told her that I would talk to Doris and call her back in just a few minutes.

Doris and sat down on the living-room sofa to discuss what plans should be made right now. We didn't know what to do. I really didn't have any time coming to me at work (vacation time was all used up), and Doris was short of cash because she had just moved into Corona with me. And then both of us said together, "We need to go now."

I called Southwest Airlines and told the lady on the other end of the phone our situation. She said that we could leave on a plane the next morning about 5:00 a.m. We booked that flight. We charged all the expenses to our Visa cards, and we began to pack. We had a two-hour drive to LAX Airport. It was now about 11:00 p.m., and we set the alarm for 3:00 a.m. We lay down for a little while. I didn't sleep; I don't think Doris slept either.

We left Corona at 3:00 a.m. There was no traffic at that time in the morning, so we made the plane just fine. We were in Denver in three hours, rented a car, and headed for the Memorial Hospital in downtown Denver. It was now about 11:00 a.m. Colorado time, and we had not eaten. We just wanted to see Jo as soon as possible. We found her room on the fourth floor ICU.

When she saw us, tears came to her eyes. Doris and I were both crying by now. We just hugged and kissed her a lot and told her how much we loved her and that we had come to pray for her and help her through this transmission. No one had said she was going to die, but we knew the end was close. None of us spoke about it. We just prayed with her, held her hand, and waited for her family to arrive. I had called Dorothy and told her we were at the hospital. Bill and Susan (Jo's son and daughter-in-law), Roxanne (Jo's oldest daughter), and Dorothy were on their way. We did not call Tom, Jo's husband. We knew the kids would tell him.

Jo said, "You're so sweet to come all this way. What about your job, Lois?" Jo never thought of herself. She was the most unselfish person I had known in my lifetime. She was my sister, and of course, I am partial, but this is the truth without a doubt.

I said, "Jo, I can get another job, but you're my sister. I want to be with you. I need to be with you. When you get out of here, you're going to need our help for a few days, so we're just getting a jump start on it." Jo said, "Lois, I am not leaving this hospital again to go to my Denver home. I am going to my heavenly home very soon. Jesus is calling my name." Doris said, "No, Jo, the doctors said that you're going to get better." Jo was short of breath. She was speaking very softly, and she gave us a little smile said, "Now, don't you pray me back, do you hear me? I am ready to go. I am tired. My purpose on this earth is done." We could see that she was in some pain. She was straining just to speak. She shut her eyes and fell asleep. Doris and I just stood there crying, not able to speak a word. We just sat by quietly for maybe fifteen minutes, and a nurse came in to check on Jo.

Doris and I left the room, and Doris decided she needed some coffee, so she went to find the cafeteria. I found a phone to call Home Depot in Corona to tell my manager where I was and why I would not be at work. My manager was very understanding. He said, "Take all the time that you need." Then I just sat down and waited for Jo's kids in the family waiting room. I wasn't there more than ten minutes when they came in. We all hugged one another and sat down to talk about Jo and what the family wanted to do.

Dotti said, "When my mom comes home, we will need to make special arrangements for a hospital bed." I was surprised that she said this after talking with Jo, and I knew Jo wasn't planning on going home, but I didn't say anything. I just let Billy, Roxanne, and Dotti say everything that they needed to talk about. Roxanne asked me where we plan on spending the night. I said, "I haven't even thought about that, but maybe we can find a motel close to the hospital." "No," she said, "I want you to stay with me. Mark and I have plenty of room." "Okay," I said, "that would be great." Her home was about twenty minutes from the hospital. Doris brought some food and coffee into the waiting room, laid everything on the table, gave hugs to everyone, and joined in the conversation.

We talked about an hour. Tom had not come in yet, and finally I couldn't keep quiet a minute longer. I said, "Kids, what if Jo can't go home? What if the Lord calls her home this time?" Dotti started to cry and said, "No, Aunt Lois, Mom is coming home. The doctors didn't say she was going to die for sure." I turned to Billy and asked, "Billy, have you talked to your dad about any plans if the doctor is wrong?" "No, Aunt Lois, Dad won't talk about it. He can't face that possibility yet. Was not going to say anything about that. We will wait and let Dad tell us when he talks to the doctors today."

We saw Tom in the hallway. He didn't stop to say hello to us, and he just went to Jo's room and stayed with her for over an hour. A few friends from the church stopped by to pray with the family and to give whatever support they could to give. Alice came. She was one of Jo's best friends. The pastor from Jo and Tom's church came. He also just wanted to pray. He went into Jo's room. Tom was still in there. They were alone for about fifteen minutes. Then the pastor came out and spoke with the kids, greeted Doris and me, and then left.

When Tom came out of Jo's room, we could see that he had been crying. He was a very private, quiet man, and this was so horrible for him. *Torture* is a perfect word. Jo and Tom had been married for forty-five years. He gave Doris and me a hug and said, "Thanks for coming. I know that Jo appreciated your being here." Doris said, "Tom, what can we do for you?" He just shook his head and said, "Nothing, thanks, I'll see you all later." And he turned and walked out of the waiting room and out of the hospital. He didn't say where he was going or how long he would be gone.

Since Jo was sleeping, we decided to go get lunch and come back later. We all walked down to the cafeteria. We all took turns sitting by Jo's bedside for the rest of that day. By 7:00 p.m., we were so tired—the flight, the emotions, the worry. We needed some sleep, so Doris and I drove to Roxanne's. Roxanne had already left to pick up her daughter from school, so we met her at the house and were happy to finally lie down and go to sleep.

The next morning, Doris and I were up at first light, took a quick shower, and were dressed, ready to go back to the hospital. We arrived there about 8:00 a.m. The nurse was with Jo, and when we walked in quietly, slowly she smiled and said, "Hi, your Jo's sisters, right?" We said, yes. She said, "She didn't have a good night. We've increased the morphine. It will help her sleep. She won't be talking much." We asked when the doctor would be coming. She said, "Soon."

Tom came into the room almost two minutes after we arrived. He gave Jo a kiss and said good morning to us. We asked him if he had slept. He didn't answer us and just kept looking at Jo and holding her hand. The nurse again repeated her report about Jo's night. She said, "The doctor will be in soon to talk with you." Tom just nodded his head and began to pray quietly by her bedside. Doris and I stepped out into the hall. We didn't want him to see us crying. He was dealing with so much pain himself; we didn't want him concerned for us in any way.

Tom came out into the hall after about twenty minutes. We said, "Could we talk for a few minutes?" He said, "Sure," and we went into the family lounge. It was just the three of us, so we felt we could ask a couple of questions. "Tom, what has the doctor told you?" He said, "She's failing." I said, "Have you told the kids this?" He said, "No, I don't want them to give up hope or stop praying." "Tom," I said, "they need to know. They're making plans to take her home." He just slowly nodded his head. He didn't say a word. We saw the doctor in the hallway. Tom got up and walked toward Jo's room. We waited in the family lounge, and the kids started arriving one by one. First, Billy then Dotti, and in about thirty minutes, Roxanne (she had dropped off Ailea Jo, her daughter, at school, and then she came into the lounge also). We waited for Tom to come out and give us the latest report from the doctor in ICU.

Tom walked into the room, and we all stood up, not saying a word, just wanting to hear what he had to say. He, choking back the tears, said, "God is calling your mom home. No one knows how much time she has. They have increased the morphine so that she won't have so much pain. Bill, I need to see you in the hall please." Everyone was crying, and no one could talk. We knew this was coming, but it was so difficult to hear the words out of Tom's mouth. Bill talked to his dad privately, and then Tom left. He didn't say where he was going. Bill came back into the lounge and said that arrangements needed to be made. He was going to call the pastor of their church, and he would also call Jo's closest friends to tell them to come and say good-bye.

Dotti and Roxanne both went to call their husbands and to tell their children that their grandma was going to see Jesus soon. Doris and I just sat with Jo. We sat by her bed for at least two hours. We read scripture to her, prayed with her, kissed her, and held her hand.

We kept telling her we were staying, not leaving for a minute. She couldn't hear us. She was slipping into a coma, a morphine-induced coma. A constant vigil of family, grandchildren, church friends, pastor, sons-in- law, daughter-in-law was at her bedside all that day.

About 4:00 p.m., Jo's personal doctor came into the room. Billy, Susan, Dotti, Roxanne, Doris, and I were by Jo's bed. The doctor had tears in his eyes, and he said, "I am so sorry. We thought the colostomy would stop the intensity of pain and give her more time, but it just wasn't good enough. I am so sorry we couldn't do more. The nerve ends in her body are like fried wiring and causing her so much pain. We will continue to increase the morphine. We want to make her as comfortable as possible. She will go deeper and deeper into a coma. Then her heart will just stop." He looked down to the floor, shook his head slowly, and added, "She needs your prayers. Goodbye." Then he left.

At 7:00 p.m. on September 6, 1999, we stood around Jo's bed and began to sing songs: "Amazing Grace," The Old Rugged Cross," "Have Thine Own Way, Lord." We sang every song we could think of that we had sung as sisters at home in Santa Monica. We prayed that the angels would come and escort Jo into heaven. Jo had not walked since she was three years old. She told us that she couldn't wait to walk across the Jordan River and see Jesus waiting for her on the other side. We kept saying, "Jo, find Mom. Go to Mom, Jo." We knew Mom would be waiting for her; Mom had passed over a year ago in August of 1998.

We watched the heart monitor on the machine above Jo's bed, observing every heartbeat she had. Tom, Billy, Susan, Dotti, Roxanne, and Doris stepped out into the hall. Some needed water; some needed just a moment of fresh air. I stayed by Jo's bed. I don't remember why I didn't go with the rest; I just didn't want to leave her. I took her left hand, kissed it, and said with tears running down my face, "Jesus, please give me a sign that Jo is okay. Please, dear God, I need a sign that she's with you."

At that very moment, Jo opened her eyes. I took a deep breath. I couldn't move. Jo looked straight ahead, and she said, "Hi, Momma."

She closed her eyes. I knew that was my answer from God. She was with Mom in heaven; the angels were coming for her.

I went out into the hallway and told the others. Tom had come back to the hospital. We all returned to Jo's bedside immediately. Her children spoke to her, telling her, "Mom, it is okay to go." Everyone was fine here; we knew she was going to Jesus.

The monitor stopped beeping. Her heart had stopped. We all stopped breathing for that moment. She was gone; Jo had died.

We all held one another for the next ten minutes. The nurses came, saw us, and just left. Jo had lived to the age of sixty-five years old. She had outlived her doctors and nurses who were so sure she would die before her twenty-first birthday. Jo had graduated from high school with honors, graduated from Santa Monica City College, and was homecoming queen in her final year. She had gone to Riverside Baptist College, graduated, and fell in love with Tom Gorrell. She got married and gave birth to three healthy children. She was now leaving seven grandchildren. She was a Sunday school teacher, women's Bible study leader, speaker at women's conferences. She was a seamstress and made beautiful wedding and prom dresses. She crotcheted beautifully and was an amazing wife to Tom for forty-five years.

Now she was with her precious Lord and Savior. "Absent from the body, present with the Lord"—we believed this and praised God for this wonderful blessing.

Tom died in 2001. Jo, Tom and Mom are all together in heaven preparing a place for the rest of us.

Time to Say Good-bye to Marjorie Lucile

Today, May 16, 2015, at 5:00 p.m., my oldest sister Marge entered heaven to see her precious Jesus.

Marge spent her last days in Payson, Arizona, where she lived with her daughter, Mari Kay, and her grandchildren. Marge always joked about living on top of the mountain in a tin can. This was because she lived in a mobile home, and Payson is ninety-four miles northeast of Phoenix in the mountains. Marge would have celebrated her eighty-fifth birthday this year in October, but the Lord had another plan for her. She had asked us girls (sisters) to plan on coming to Payson in October to help her celebrate this milestone year.

Marge was able to spend Christmas 2014 with us in Pismo Beach with all the sisters. She was able to spend a few days with each of us before returning home. She was afraid to fly alone, so Mari was able to find her an escort to and from the plane, and she was so happy just to know she was not alone.

Marge took us to Marie Callender's restaurant for breakfast the day after our Christmas celebration; that was her gift to us. She loved Marie Callender's, and we were saddened to hear that the restaurant was closing and on this day—well, it was the last day to be open.

Marge took a fall in her mobile home sometime early in April 2015. She didn't tell anyone. She just lay around, and her back was hurting. She suffered through it for a while. Finally, she was in so much pain in her back and her stomach that Mari took her to the ER in Payson. Her stomach was extended and swollen a lot. After several x-rays, they discovered colitis and kidney injury. She stayed in the hospital for several days then was sent to a convalescent care center for ten days.

Marge was very tired, in a lot of pain, and was giving up. She just asked to go home, her heavenly home. She wanted to die in her own home. Trudy, Bill, Doris, Lou, and George drove to Payson to be with Marge for several days. Her son Jack Donald Jr. came to see her on Wednesday, April 29. He stayed three days. When he left, she was ready to call on the angels to come and get her. This was where she took her last breath, with Mari, her grandchildren, and friends at her side. This place was her palace, her home. The tin can on top of the mountain was where she took her last breath, today, May 6, 2015, at 5:00 p.m.

APPENDIX

More information about Polio and Helms Bakery
can be found online, through Google.

Family Photo 2005

First Generation 1929

Ellender and Truman Jones

Ellender & Truman Jones + 10 Kids = 12

Grand kids = 23

Great Grand Kids = 61

Great Great Grandkids = 38

134

ABOUT THE AUTHOR

 Lois Price is the ninth child of Ellender and Truman Jones. She was raised in Santa Monica, California. She is happily married with three children and eight grandchildren.

Along with her six sisters and her brother, they loved and cherished their beloved mother. She was an inspiration to all of them. They want to remember and honor her memory forever so that her grandchildren and great-grandchildren will know the wonderful person she was. She loved her Bible and trusted God in all things. She knew how important underlining scripture was and the value in praying daily for guidance.

She taught everyone to love and care for each other, until they all meet again in Heaven.